PENGUIN
EVERY DAY'S A GOOD DAY
WILLIAM PIKE

EVERY DAY'S A GOOD DAY

WILLIAM PIKE

PENGUIN BOOKS

PENGUIN BOOKS
Published by the Penguin Group
Penguin Group (NZ), 67 Apollo Drive, Rosedale, North Shore 0632, New
Zealand (a division of Pearson New Zealand Ltd)
Penguin Group (USA) Inc., 375 Hudson Street, New York,
New York 10014, USA
Penguin Group (Canada), 90 Eglinton Avenue East,
Suite 700, Toronto, Ontario, M4P 2Y3, Canada (a division of
Pearson Penguin Canada Inc.)
Penguin Books Ltd, 80 Strand, London, WC2R 0RL, England
Penguin Ireland, 25 St Stephen's Green, Dublin 2, Ireland
(a division of Penguin Books Ltd)
Penguin Group (Australia), 250 Camberwell Road,
Camberwell, Victoria 3124, Australia (a division of
Pearson Australia Group Pty Ltd)
Penguin Books India Pvt Ltd, 11, Community Centre,
Panchsheel Park, New Delhi – 110 017, India
Penguin Books (South Africa) (Pty) Ltd, 24 Sturdee Avenue, Rosebank,
Johannesburg 2196, South Africa

Penguin Books Ltd, Registered Offices: 80 Strand,
London, WC2R 0RL, England

First published by Penguin Group (NZ), 2008
1 3 5 7 9 10 8 6 4 2

Copyright © William Pike 2008

The right of William Pike to be identified as the author of this work in terms of
section 96 of the Copyright Act 1994 is hereby asserted.

Designed by Shaun Jury
Typeset by Pindar New Zealand
Printed in Australia by McPherson's Printing Group
Cover: Abseiling photograph by Doug Sherring

All rights reserved. Without limiting the rights under copyright reserved above,
no part of this publication may be reproduced, stored in or introduced into
a retrieval system, or transmitted, in any form or by any means (electronic,
mechanical, photocopying, recording or otherwise), without the prior written
permission of both the copyright owner and the above publisher of this book.

ISBN 978 014 330419 7
A catalogue record for this book is available
from the National Library of New Zealand.

www.penguin.co.nz

Acknowledgements: The publishers are grateful for permission to reproduce
copyright material. Whilst every reasonable effort has been made to trace
copyright holders, the publishers would be pleased to hear from any not
acknowledged.

This book is proudly dedicated with great love to my special Dad, Barry, my caring Mum, Tracy, and my amazing brother, Andrew.

CONTENTS

	ACKNOWLEDGEMENTS	9
	FOREWORD	15
CHAPTER ONE	DINNER ON THE ICE	17
CHAPTER TWO	ABOUT ME	26
CHAPTER THREE	INTENDED TONGARIRO TRAVERSE – DAY ONE	49
CHAPTER FOUR	OUTDOOR ACTION	66
CHAPTER FIVE	INTENDED TONGARIRO TRAVERSE – DAY TWO	84
CHAPTER SIX	EXPLORING INNER SPACE	95
CHAPTER SEVEN	MIGHTIER THAN A MOUNTAIN	112
CHAPTER EIGHT	WORDS FROM OTHERS: THE COLD HARD FACTS	128
CHAPTER NINE	CHASING DREAMS	166
CHAPTER TEN	A NEW LEASE ON LIFE	182
CHAPTER ELEVEN	HOTEL HOSPITAL	202
CHAPTER TWELVE	HOME SWEET HOME	227

EPILOGUE	236
GLOSSARY	239
RECOMMENDED READING	243
RECOMMENDED WEBSITES	246
FROM MY PARENTS	248

ACKNOWLEDGEMENTS

It's a great privilege for me to be able to acknowledge so many special, courageous, loving and talented people who were involved in my rescue on 25 September 2007 and my recovery since. I will forever be indebted to them all as, thanks to them, I am now able to live a normal life, one that may be more full and enriched than if I had not had the accident.

I'd like to name every single person involved in my rescue, care and recovery – they all deserve the highest possible recognition. However, the list would become a book on its own. So, it's only practical to acknowledge individuals generally, and major groups of people, organisations and significant individuals, without whom I would not be writing these acknowledgements.

To everyone who was involved in my rescue and recovery – please know that you made a profound impact on my life, recovery and ability to keep positive in times that seemed nothing but overwhelmingly negative. The words 'rescue' and 'recovery' are used in a broad sense to mean both those who had a hands-on, direct influence on my rescue and recovery, and everyone else who I communicated with in hospital and afterwards. Regardless of whether your thoughts were simply with me, or you sent a postcard, email or picked up the phone to share your sympathy – that was enough. For every single person who took the time to drive or fly to Waikato Hospital, words cannot explain how much joy I was filled with to see your caring faces.

I'd also like to deeply thank those who came to comfort and assist Mum, Dad and Andrew in times of difficulty. Your actions not only helped them immensely by keeping them sane, but also enabled them to do their best in encouraging me back to normal health.

Dad, Mum and Andrew – you mean more than the world to me. I'm still surprised at how composed you have been since my accident. You went way beyond the call of duty to care for me, but that's who you are and what makes you three so special to me. I'm so lucky to have you in my life. From the beginning you have set me up to live a special life and then guided me to continue living that life – no one else could ever give me anything as grand as that. Mum – thanks for keeping diaries throughout hospital and afterwards. If I ever need to be brought back to reality or stop complaining about something, I'll just read those diaries.

Without you and the rest of our extended family all pulling together to support me, my ability to keep a positive outlook on my life-changing situation would have been severely impaired. The brave faces you all put on to mask your grief and fear are unbelievable and honourable. When I needed you most, you were always there, and when I didn't need you – or thought I didn't need you, but did! – you were always there. The hours you spent by my bedside will never be forgotten. You all know who you are, and thank you to those who made the effort. You will never be alone if you end up in hospital.

Without family and friends you have nothing. I'm so fortunate to have a bunch of friends who have stood by me before, during and after my accident. Whenever someone asks me, 'William, how did you stay strong after your accident?' I always answer with, 'I've got such a supportive bunch of friends . . .' and I really mean it. Thanks for being there guys 'n' girls – you've helped me amazingly.

James Christie – it's been said before and I'll say it again: you are much more than just a mate, you are my hero. Without your brave actions on Mt Ruapehu, I would surely be dead. But you are not only *my* hero. I strongly believe you are a hero to everyone who knows me and you; and you are one of New Zealand's heroes – you deserve a medal. As a quiet, perhaps reluctant, hero, don't ever play down the enormity of your heroism. A lesser person may have broken down under the pressure of the fears and dangers you experienced. You started the ball rolling to give me a second chance at life, and the second chance you gave me has been the most interesting journey in my life so far – that is the ultimate gift.

I have unconditional confidence in New Zealand's Department of Conservation (DOC). To me DOC is a symbol of New Zealand's outdoors, and the people who work for DOC are stereotypical 'good old Kiwis'. DOC as a whole do an amazing job in maintaining the outdoors for all to safely enjoy. They do this for us now and also with forethought for those of the future. Bhrent Guy and his team from the Tongariro National Park Visitors' Centre (Whakapapa) deserve recognition and huge thanks for initially co-ordinating the search and rescue, then seeing it through until I was met by ambulance officers. Your continued communication with me and my family, and James and his family, is greatly appreciated.

The people of the Ruapehu Alpine Rescue Organisation (RARO) are the lifeguards of the mountain. They are a tight-knit team of courageous, dedicated, experienced and highly skilled professionals whose job is to go beyond what DOC, the New Zealand Police and other search and rescue teams are capable of. To rescue me, RARO members Phil

Smith, Andy Hoyle, Nicky Hughes, Murray McErlich, Shane Buckingham, Reto Sporrer, Callum Learmouth and Mark Woods far exceeded their job requirements by putting their lives in danger. Although they calculated and controlled the risk to themselves as much as possible, the unknown volcanic risk was massive. I'll never be able to thank you all enough, but I'll try – thanks team!

It means a lot to me to publicly acknowledge and thank the two helicopter crews who kept me alive en-route to Taumarunui and Waikato Hospitals. Firstly, the Taupo Lion Foundation Helicopter with pilot Dan Harcourt, advanced paramedic Graeme Taylor and crewman Barry Shepherd. Secondly, the Westpac Waikato Air Ambulance Helicopter with pilot Simon Lewis, advanced paramedic Paula John and Dr John Bonning, specialist emergency physician. Both crews are very talented, highly skilled and exceptionally likeable people. If it wasn't for your actions and the Westpac Rescue Helicopter network, I wouldn't be alive today.

I have nothing but praise for Waikato Hospital and its staff. My hospital stay was made as pleasant as possible by every staff member who had anything to do with my case. My room was always clean, I was fed like a king, doctors and nurses did a fantastic job and the surgeons are top-notch. I couldn't have asked for anything more; keep it up! So, thank you nurses, doctors, cooks, cleaners, trauma team, communications, orderlies, orthopaedics, plastics, physiotherapists, occupational therapists and all the others who made an infinite impression on my life.

The following organisations and people have also had a significant role in my rescue, recovery and future: Clevedon School – students, teachers and parents; everyone at the Penguin Group; New Zealand Police; Taumarunui Hospital; Taumarunui ambulance officers Jo-ann Malcolm and John Semmes; Chateau Tongariro (those who filled hot-water

ACKNOWLEDGEMENTS

bottles, lent a hand in the middle of the night and gave James a place to rest); the New Zealand media; various volunteers who helped save my life; the New Zealand Blood Service; the New Zealand Artificial Limb Board; Millennium Institute of Sport and Health; Accident Compensation Corporation (ACC) – in particular Nigel Swain; Ergowise – in particular Elise Bergeron; North Shore Hospital – in particular Mark Crainswick; North Sport Water Polo; Nigel Blanchard of Prytex Outdoors Ltd for sponsoring me with Mountain Equipment, Extremities and Terra Nova outdoor equipment.

The combined effort of everyone mentioned above greatly improved my chances of survival and the continuation of my recovery to lead a normal life again. Lastly, I'd like to thank those people I phoned, emailed or spoke to who gave me ideas or recommendations for this book.

William Pike
May 2008

FOREWORD

We all remember where we were when significant things in life happen. I clearly remember my birthday on the 27th of September 2007, not because it was my birthday, but because a young mountaineer had just experienced what I was sure would become a defining few days in his life – that is, if he survived them.

At about 8 p.m. on 25 September, William's life changed in an instant in the Dome Shelter near the summit of Mt Ruapehu. Reading his words, and those of the people who battled for him, brought back to me so many memories of how my life changed in late 1982 when, after thirteen and a half days stuck in an ice cave on the summit of Mt Cook/Aoraki, I had both legs amputated below the knee.

Give some thought to this: it took me twenty years to write a book about that hiccup to my climbing career and the opportunities that being able to live a different life brought – it has taken William less than twenty weeks! This should give you an insight into the story of William's life so far and hint at what he will achieve in the exciting future ahead.

One statement in this book defines William and his story to me: '. . . only one leg had been amputated – that's better than two!'

This sums up his attitude, his desire not just to survive, but to excel! What many will see as a tragedy, he has analysed, understood and embraced as the opportunity to lead a new life, to accept and revel in the challenges ahead.

Every Day's a Good Day is required reading for everyone who has gone through or is going through trauma, be it an accident or illness – in fact, this book should be read by everyone, because we can all gain strength and motivation from William's example.

William has redefined the concept of a positive attitude and what focus really means!

Mark Inglis
Hanmer Springs, May 2008

CHAPTER ONE

DINNER ON THE ICE

*The best climber in the world is the
one who's having the most fun.*
ALEX LOWE

Wearing my thick gloves, I carefully lifted the lid from my cooking pot with my thumb and index finger. Steam billowed from the pot preventing me from seeing the macaroni cheese that had been simmering for the past few minutes. A bitterly cold breeze was bending around the leeward side of the Dome Shelter, making my eyes water and numbing my nose. My eyes and nose were the only parts of my entire body that were exposed to the harsh mountain environment. I was standing outside the Dome Shelter, a hut that is very close to the crater lake on Mt Ruapehu, which at 2792 metres is the highest mountain in the North Island of New Zealand. The Dome Shelter is 2672 metres above sea level.

I was on the northern side of the Dome Shelter cooking dinner for my friend, James, and me. The wind chill was about -10°C and the air temperature was well below zero. It was 6.30 p.m. on 25 September 2007. James was inside the shelter reorganising the clutter of equipment the pair of us had dumped there, while I kept a close eye on dinner. I was proud of myself for having carved out a makeshift kitchen bench within the ice that had completely encased the Dome Shelter. With my ice axe, I chipped into the thick ice to make a flat spot for my stove and cooking pots to sit. I even added a small lip around the edge to stop anything sliding off the 'bench' onto the snow and down a steep snow bank that was a few metres behind me. I made the lip from snow that I squeezed in my gloved hands, shaping it like Play-Doh.

For a brief moment I turned my back to my home-made kitchen and took a look at the enormity of the summit plateau. My feet were starting to get very cold from standing still but I tried not to think about it.

The summit plateau is a massive flat area of snow and ice to the north of the Dome Shelter, stretching over one square kilometre. That means if you placed a huge square over the summit plateau, each side of the square would need to be over 1000 metres long – it's that huge.

It was a stunning sight in the fading light. I could have stood there looking at the summit plateau forever but I was distracted by the bubbling and boiling sound of our dinner. I spun around just in time to lift the lid off the pot and stop the precious contents from boiling over and staining the pure white snow and ice.

The frigid air rapidly cooled the pasta and the steam disappeared. Dinner was ready and it looked so tasty. The second I turned the roaring hot stove off, the cooking pot immediately began to cool. I left the stove on the bench and walked around to the shelter's entrance, being careful not to slip on the ice.

The Dome Shelter is exactly as it's named; a shelter on a dome-shaped hill that's covered in snow. Well, in winter at least – in summer, there's no snow and it's all rock. Think of a dome shape as a soccer ball cut in half and placed on the ground. The shelter is a small and simple building, and – no prizes for guessing – it provides shelter from the weather. It has no windows, no beds, no electricity, no running water, no kitchen sink, no toilet and no heating. What does it have then? One seat and a spade. Cool, eh?! The hut houses three rooms. The first two rooms each measure about three metres by one and a half metres. The third room is bigger but not by much – it would be around three metres by three metres.

When James and I arrived at the hut earlier in the day, the door was three-quarters buried with powdery snow. With our shovels, we dug the door out and shaped steps from the snow down into the shelter to make it easier to get in and out. An alternative entrance into the hut is the escape hatch, similar to a short fat chimney. A ladder inside the first room begins at the floor and climbs up into the chimney. When the main entrance is blocked with bullet-proof ice, hopefully the escape hatch isn't!

Carrying our dinner, I managed to negotiate the slippery ice and walk down the crumbly snow steps to the shelter's door. Inside the shelter it was pitch dark, so I flicked my headlamp on as I closed the door. James was sitting in the second room on the hut's one seat. He looked cold. The pasta was getting colder by the second, so I gave James the pot, while I wedged a shovel between the two walls as a sort of seat for me.

James peered into the pot, letting the hot steam rise and warm his face. He then stirred a sachet of plain tuna into the macaroni cheese. Having made his addition to our dinner, James eagerly spooned half the pot of macaroni cheese onto his plate. He passed my cooking pot over to me and I wolfed the pasta straight from the pot – there's less dishes that way!

I looked across to James and thought how much we looked like Antarctic explorers wrapped from head to toe in our various layers of clothing. We wore balaclavas, long-sleeved and long-legged thermals next to our skin, fleece jackets on top of our thermals, down jackets on top of those, and then water and windproof jackets and pants to top off the outfit. We also had thick ski gloves on our hands.

We didn't talk for a few minutes; we were too busy stuffing our faces. I'm sure it can't be good for you to eat that quickly but we didn't care. That pasta was so good, even the last little bit that was stone cold. I couldn't bear to waste even the tiniest bit – each spoonful supplied valuable carbohydrates and protein that would help my body recover from today's strenuous climb and fuel me for tomorrow's long walk to the Tama Lakes, which are on the saddle between Mt Ruapehu and Mt Ngauruhoe.

While I still had all my protective clothing on, I decided to go outside and snap a few photos in the last of the dwindling sunset. Sitting on the shovel, I strapped on my crampons and then grabbed my ice axe from the corner of the hut. On my way out I took my camera off the nail I'd hung it on and stashed my tripod in my jacket pocket. James kindly offered to wash the dishes and tidy up the hut ready for sleep while I was out. Washing dishes in the mountains is easy. All you need to do is scoop up snow with the cooking pot and furiously rub the snow against the dirty surface of the cutlery and the pot. Any leftovers in the pot will freeze instantly and come off, leaving you with pretty clean dishes.

I peeled back the four layers of clothing to check my watch. It was 7.30 p.m. Once I got outside, the cold was bone numbing and it was extremely icy underfoot. My crampons made a distinct crunch, crunch noise as the spikes pierced the glass-hard ice. A steady wind blew against my back as I walked towards the top of the Dome. Looking out to the west, the sun had completely disappeared and its light had been replaced by the full moon, casting a silver glow over everything I could see. The moonlight was so bright that I turned off my headlamp as I approached the highest point of the Dome. Once I got to the top, I stood statue-still, then turned in a 360-degree circle to survey the horizon. It was breathtaking. I thought to myself, Gee, New Zealand *is* actually the most beautiful place on this earth.

Words can hardly describe how I felt, but I'll give it a go! I had shivers trickling up and down my spine. I felt *awesome*. And I was so happy. Happy to be alive, fit, healthy and experiencing this mind-blowing view thanks to a sport that I had truly fallen in love with: mountaineering. Every day was a good day; I loved life and I loved the mountains. I honestly couldn't have been in a better place, I was in paradise. I was on a high – high up on Mt Ruapehu, a perfect place to be.

Reality soon hit though, when my feet started to feel a bit cold, momentarily distracting me from my overwhelming feeling of happiness.

I slowly made my way back over the crunching ice, thinking about the Dome Shelter, which, within seconds, I'd be safe inside. I was looking forward to rolling out my bed mat and wriggling into my toasty-warm sleeping bag ready for a perfect night's sleep, after a perfect day on the mountain.

At the bottom of the snow stairs in front of the shelter's door, I clicked my headlamp on again, went inside and firmly shut the door. Actually, I closed it so firmly that I thought I should check that I could open it again. I tried and couldn't get it open, even after pulling the handle as hard as I could!

While I struggled with the door, I could hear James laughing at me. Eventually he passed me a spade so I could try prying the door open but no luck, it stayed firmly shut. When that didn't work, I reluctantly swung my ice axe into the door and yanked on it. Finally, it swung open! Happy to have solved my problem, I closed the door again and decided that I'd worry about opening it again in the morning.

Earlier on, James and I had agreed to sleep in the room closest to the main entrance. The room behind us, which ran parallel to the one we were in, housed a generator and stank of diesel from the generator. I didn't want to wake with a headache, or worse still, not wake up from the lethal fumes.

James had already laid his sleeping mat and sleeping bag on the floor of the hut. I quickly undid my crampons and placed them neatly in the corner of the hut. I pulled my sleeping bag out of my pack then unravelled my thin blue sleeping mat. The sight of my sleeping mat always makes me cringe at the thought of the hard night's sleep to come. I don't think you can call them mattresses when they're only one centimetre thick. As uncomfortable as they are, they do the trick by acting as insulation between the cold floor and sleeping bag. Plus, they're as light as a feather and ideal for hauling up mountains.

With my sleeping bag and mat in place I started the chilly task of getting undressed. I hung my jacket and pants on a nail then stuffed my down jacket into my sleeping-bag bag. The jacket-stuffed bag makes a great pillow. I got into my sleeping bag with my headlamp still on. I was wearing my underwear and my polyprops – a long-sleeved top and long-legged pants. On my feet I wore a pair of super-thin sock liners, made from a quick-drying material.

Every time I breathed out through my mouth or nose, my headlamp's beam illuminated the warmed air, making it look as though I were smoking a cigarette.

Once in bed, James and I had a brief debate over what time we'd wake up. 'I'm keen to get up at 4.30, we can have a quick brekky and catch the sunrise as we're walking. I wanna take a few photos. What do you reckon?'

James twisted his face and shrieked, '4.30?! No way. How about 6? The sun still won't even be up then.'

I tried to compromise and said, 'Well . . . how about 5.30? It'll give us plenty of time.'

'All right then,' James replied. 'I'll set my alarm and you set yours too.'

I knew I'd be awake around 4.30 anyway, lying in my sleeping bag, excited and itching to get up and get going. But you never know, I might sleep in so I said, 'Sweet, you've got a deal.'

As I lay there reading an outdoors magazine I'd brought with me, I turned my cell phone on and discovered it had reception. I texted my friend Cameron to ask him for a weather forecast for the next day. A few minutes later he texted me back with an update. Incredible really, when you think about it, that I could be snuggled up in a hut near the top of Mt Ruapehu and still be in touch with the world!

'Good news, James, the weather report is fantastic for tomorrow. Fine, light winds, freezing level 1800 metres,' I reported.

'Awesome!' was James's reply.

I was so excited I wondered how on earth I'd get to sleep now.

I said goodnight to James and lay on my back in my sleeping bag with my arms tightly at my side to keep me warm. With my eyes shut, I lay there thinking about what a great day we'd had. That led me on to thinking about how fantastic tomorrow would be, with the fine weather and a challenging adventure ahead. The next leg of our planned trip was going to take us somewhere I'd never been before, and I liked it that way.

I looked at my watch. It was 8 p.m. A pretty early night, I thought.

I'd been really tired over the past few weeks because I'd been working late on assignments, so I relished the thought of nine and a half hours of warm, cosy and uninterrupted sleep.

A few minutes later, half asleep, half awake, I felt a shudder tremble through my body. It was kind of like what I thought an earthquake would be like, except I'd never experienced one before so I wasn't entirely sure. It was really quiet. I wondered if it was a small avalanche in the far distance. However, that didn't seem right. Avalanches don't usually happen at night, in fine weather and when it's so cold. I was puzzled.

What unfolded over the next few minutes would change my life forever.

No more than two seconds after the initial shudder, the main door of the hut blew open with frightening force. What the heck? Is someone playing a joke?

Still inside my sleeping bag, I got up and knelt in front of the now wide-open door. I grasped either side of the door frame with my bare hands and poked my head out the door. The sight before my eyes is one I'll never forget. It looked like a swarm of trillions and trillions of bumblebees speeding across the sky. Except this swarm contained objects much larger than bees. If only it had been bees that began to sting my face and not rubble from a volcano.

Frightened to death I screamed, 'James! The mountain is erupting!'

In that same instant, hurricane-strength winds carrying volcanic rock, mud and water bashed into the right-hand side of my face and body. They were actually travelling faster than the speed of sound. I could have been shot in the face with a machine gun and not known the difference. I tried to close the door but a mightier force blew it open again.

Before I could think, move or say anything else everything went pitch black. In the darkness my lower body was punished. Unknown to me, the muddy water that was flowing swiftly into the hut was effortlessly carrying rocks the size of ten-litre buckets and bigger. The rocks came through the main door with such speed, they were like bowling balls hurtling down a bowling alley, knocking the skittles out of their way. My legs became the skittles and weren't so much knocked over as smashed to bits. The impact of the rocks hitting my lower legs was like nothing I had ever experienced before. It was similar to a huge steam roller slowly squeezing the life out of my legs, bursting veins, arteries and blood vessels like fragile balloons. Bones were smashed and splintered. I was completely helpless, waiting for whatever was crushing me to kill me.

In the inky-black darkness, I could only feel what was happening to me and not see it.

Water started to fill the hut. I first felt it swirling around my waist and then realised it was swiftly rising. A terrible thought crossed my mind. Was I going to drown? In a desperate attempt to free myself I began to thrash around with all the energy I could muster, kind of like a great white shark with a hook in its mouth. I did not want this to be the end – it was too soon. I did not want to die like this. My struggle to keep my head above the water failed as a foul-tasting liquid started to lap around my mouth, ears, nose and eyes.

I thought I was about to die. What would it be like to be dead? What have I done to deserve to die this way? What would my family and friends be thinking at my funeral as I was put to eternal rest under two metres of cold, heavy soil?

CHAPTER TWO

ABOUT ME

Every day's a good day
WILLIAM PIKE

One afternoon when I was visiting my grandparents, Grandad sat me down on the couch.

'William,' he said, 'I have something ask you.'

Straight away, I thought I was in trouble. Was he going to ask me if I had been shooting sparrows with his air gun again? Or if I had been shooting it at the old lady's house next door? Or if I had eaten the remainder of the chocolate biscuits in the cupboard?

Luckily it was none of the above. Instead he said, 'William, I have always wanted to go to Nepal and I've spoken to your parents about taking you with me. Would you like to come on a three-week trip to Nepal with me?'

I was a bit confused.

'Go in a pool for three weeks?' He's losing it, I thought. I'd come out more wrinkled than both Grandma and Grandad put together.

'What pool, Grandad, what do you mean?' I asked.

Grandad was quick to correct my misunderstanding.

'No, no, not a pool. Ne-pal. Nepal, you know, Mt Everest. Mt Everest is in Nepal.'

I knew Mt Everest was the highest mountain in the world, but I had no idea it was in Nepal or where Nepal even was.

ABOUT ME

I fired off some question as to Nepal's whereabouts. I wanted to be sure I wasn't going to spend three weeks in a pool. Within a minute Grandad had several atlases spread out on the coffee table.

Soon I had a pretty good idea where we were going, and was relieved that it had nothing to do with pools.

As I stared at the atlas, I started to feel excited. We would have to fly to Nepal and I had never been in an aeroplane before. It didn't matter what was in Nepal, I was excited enough about the aeroplane ride!

I was only eleven years old when Grandad asked me to go with him to Nepal, but I would be twelve by the time we left. Luckily for me, my grandad is a really adventurous, inquisitive and generous person, otherwise my chances of going on such an exciting trip would have been very slim.

Grandad was originally from England, and had done a lot of exploring in the English countryside before he moved to New Zealand. Once he and Grandma moved to New Zealand, he enjoyed exploring this country too. The idea of a trip to Nepal was very appealing to the explorer in him.

I did some research of my own at the school library and began to realise that Nepal would be very different from New Zealand. I learned that Nepal had huge mountain ranges, that the landscape was at a much higher altitude than New Zealand and that people from Nepal were generally poor and worked very hard for very little.

For the next six months I tried to tuck away my excitement about the Nepal trip in the back of my mind. Whenever I saw a mountain, an aeroplane or Grandad, I began to think more and more about leaving for Nepal. I was getting seriously excited and a little bit nervous. I was nervous about a few things. I had to have immunisations to prevent me from catching certain diseases and I hate injections (always have and always will!). I was also nervous because I'd been told that there were deadly snakes and spiders in some of the places we were visiting.

On 12 April 1997, I finally boarded an aeroplane for the first time. It was like stepping onto a high-tech spaceship for me. The best part out of the trip was the take off. The way I was thrown back into my seat when the aeroplane was at full throttle was exhilarating. The next best part of the trip was going up into the cockpit while en route to our first stop-over, Brisbane, in Australia. Grandad told an air hostess that I had never been on an aeroplane before so she walked me up to the cockpit door, knocked on the door, and the two pilots welcomed me in – I was so lucky!

From Brisbane we flew to Bangkok in Thailand. When I stepped off the aeroplane the heat nearly knocked me off my feet. I couldn't believe how hot it was. I was shocked at the conditions in which some of the people lived in Bangkok. It really made me appreciate my everyday life in Auckland.

After five days in Bangkok, we finally got on the plane to fly to Kathmandu, the capital of Nepal. When I got off the aeroplane in Nepal, it wasn't quite as hot as Bangkok, thankfully.

During our three weeks in Nepal, we got to see a lot of things. I got to see – and take photos of – one of the biggest tourist attractions in the world, Mt Everest!

To get there, we flew in a huge twin-rotor helicopter from Kathmandu to the Shyangboche landing strip. From there we walked a short distance to the Hotel Everest View. It's no surprise that from the hotel there is a splendid view of Mt Everest standing staunch at 8848 metres.

I really enjoyed travelling through Nepal. Before going there, I didn't really understand that people *do* live very differently from the way we do in little old New Zealand. The huge contrast in culture and living standards made me appreciate New Zealand so much more.

I was shocked to see a row of bodies lined up on the side

of a river in Pashupatinath. The bodies were cremated in an open fire, and when the remains burnt down to embers, a man would sweep the ashes into the river, ready for the next cremation. While it seemed strange to me, this kind of cremation ritual is part of the Hindu tradition in the area.

Towards the end of our amazing trip, we visited the Royal Chitwan National Park. In an unstable boat we crossed one of the rivers bordering the wildlife park, past a few sunbathing hippopotamus. Once on the island we were whisked into a small room for an island safety talk.

I prepared myself for another stock-standard, boring safety talk. By using common sense you'd be able to keep yourself out of any dangerous situations.

I was immediately startled. A staff member began explaining, in broken Engligh, that there is no fencing keeping wildlife from wandering past our bungalows and we would be sharing the park with the wildlife.

That's OK, I thought, until the staff member started to mention . . .

'Wildlife to watch out for are: rhinoceros, crocodiles, elephants, antelopes, striped hyenas, lizards, pythons, cobras, green pit vipers, tortoises, common leopards, wild dogs and monkeys, and much more!'

That's totally wicked! I remember thinking.

I couldn't believe that there were all those deadly animals right outside where we were sleeping. The staff member recommended not travelling between each other's rooms at night time – understandable and fair enough! He also recommended checking our shoes, shower, bed sheets and toilet seat for poisonous spiders at all times.

From that moment on I became really cautious and my eyes began to play cruel jokes with me. Everything I spotted that looked remotely like a spider made me jump and I checked *everything* for spiders!

Over the next few days we went elephant riding and rhinoceros spotting and also did some small walks around the park to spot the countless mammals, reptiles and amphibious animals.

Our guide for spotting rhinoceros made sure we didn't wear any bright clothing, as rhinoceros tend to charge at bright colours. If a rhinoceros were to charge, our guide said to 'run fast as you can, climb tree like fast monkey and wait for me.' That was really reassuring. Not!

We did see a few rhinos. What amazing, beastly creatures. They were massive, and so impressively built with their intimidating horn and armour cladding that made them look like invincible tanks.

After our wild time at the wildlife park we travelled through Nepalese towns and gained superb views of the Himalayas. The Himalayan mountains tower higher into the sky than anything else I have ever seen. I can't say for sure that it was seeing the Himalayas that made me want to become a mountaineer. Perhaps they were indirectly responsible for igniting my passion for mountaineering. I'd say it was a combination of both visiting Nepal and going on dozens of tramping trips, and eventually my first mountaineering trip, that got me hooked.

I was born on 7 January 1985 at 6.18 p.m. at National Women's Hospital in Auckland. From there my mum and dad brought me back to their newly purchased house in Glenfield on the North Shore of Auckland.

My earliest memories of our house in Glenfield are of building a tree hut in a huge gum tree. I used to nail bits of firewood to the gum tree in the backyard. The hut, as you might imagine, wasn't like a small house or shed with a roof. This hut was nowhere near that classy! It had a few seats and a couple of shelves for things to be stored on. If I was lucky enough, Mum would bring me lunch in the tree hut – that was something special! Hundreds-and-thousands biscuits, Marmite and cheese sandwiches, and tomato sauce with cheerio sausages (not cheerios with tomato sauce – I love tomato sauce!) were some of the special treats I remember!

Even though the hut might not have been the best in the neighbourhood, it sure was colourful, because Mum would bring home free test pots from the local paint shop. Test pots are supposed to be used for testing to see whether the colour of paint you like looks all right on what you're painting and test them out, I did! Every piece of wood that didn't belong to the tree was the colour of a rainbow.

The tree hut was a good lookout to the next door neighbours' property and I could monitor their every movement, pretending to be James Bond 007. I used to hang out with the boy from next door. He was a year older than me and a little unpredictable. Some days he'd be friendly, some days he wouldn't want anything to do with me.

At the end of one long day I had finished building a real birdhouse with my dad and felt very proud of myself. The birdhouse was made of thick plywood and looked just like a bought one. The nails were neat, the wood joined up nicely, and it had a wooden pole for the birds to land on, so they could then enter the house through a round hole in the wood.

Overnight, I left it on the ground next to the hedge separating our section from the neighbours'. The next day I planned to make it a snazzy addition to my tree hut. The thought of a few pet birds in my tree hut had me fizzing with excitement.

I woke up early the next morning and couldn't wait to take my birdhouse up to my tree hut. To my horror, when I went to pick the birdhouse up, I noticed the wooden pole for the birds to land on had been snapped off. It was a little thicker than a pencil, and had to have been broken by someone or something. I was so upset.

The next time I saw my so-called mate, I asked him whether he knew anything about my birdhouse being broken. As I recall, he owned up to breaking it and he didn't even say sorry. I just couldn't understand why someone would do that. From then on, I decided not to have anything to do with him. I thought about taking revenge, but realised that would make me as nasty as he was. Mum always told me that two wrongs don't make a right and this was definitely a time when that was true. It didn't stop me from hanging out in my tree house and spying on him though! In between building my tree hut and spying on my nasty neighbour, I made beer.

Making beer was a fine art that took time, patience and precision. I wheeled my red plastic wheelbarrow to a small area of bush in the corner of our property. Taking as much time as required, I used to dig into the ground with my plastic spade, finding and separating the different layers of soil and clay into neat piles. If the soil was in good condition, not too wet, not too dry, I would have four different categories: stick 'n' leaves, top soil (with worms if I was lucky), black soil and clay.

The precision for a fine brew of beer came in the form of bark from Mum's garden. She still doesn't know where her bark disappeared to. Bark was a key ingredient in beer and patience was required to get just the right mix. The four types of soil were standard in every batch of beer and any batch with worms was classed as a limited edition. Once I was satisfied with separating enough ingredients, I would shovel the perfect amount of each ingredient into my wheelbarrow. The finishing touch was water added from the garden hose, and then the brew was stirred with my shovel. Mmmm, wouldn't you love a sip of my beer?

When it was too hot to make beer, I'd be splashing around

in the paddling pool in our backyard. Year after year Mum and Dad would buy a cheap paddling pool made from a blue nylon material similar to a tarpaulin. It was held in a square shape with a metal frame, with sides about thirty centimetres high. I'd spend hours upon hours in the paddling pool each day. Every day the paddling pool would need to be emptied and refilled due to the amount of grass and grit picked up by my feet and deposited into the water. Towards the end of every summer, somehow the pool would end up with a hole in it, usually too big to repair. Was it caused by my wheelbarrow, spade, snorkelling equipment or bike? I'll never know.

Only when the sun was low in the sky and the air began to cool off would I go inside and flick on the television for the only programme I watched. I didn't watch much television, I found it boring, except for that one programme about a father and his daughter who lived on a boat and went scuba diving all the time. I'd sit there absolutely entranced watching the series that was so full of action and adventure.

I reckon the combination of the paddling pool and my favourite television series saw the beginning of my love for the ocean.

After watching *Sea Hunt* I would go for a scuba dive before bed. Being only four or five years old, there's no way I could afford scuba diving gear, nor were my parents going to buy the expensive equipment. So, a little creativeness and improvisation was all that was needed.

I had a three-litre juice bottle with shoulder straps made from thin strips of elastic. I'd strap that to my back as a dive cylinder. I used swimming goggles instead of a real diving mask, even though they only covered my eyes and not my nose. I'd have a drinking straw sticking out of my mouth as my regulator. With rubber fins on, I would crawl down the hallway on my stomach, pretending to be scuba diving with my dive cylinder (juice bottle), regulator (straw), dive mask (swimming goggles) and swimming fins. What a clown!

My crazy obsession with scuba diving didn't stop at the end of the hallway. In fact, that was just the start of it! At the end of the hallway, I'd hang a right into the bathroom – and then the fun would begin.

Still dressed as a scuba diver, I'd spend at least half an hour in the bath. After a while I'd get a little bored with staring through my swimming goggles at the white and silver plug hole that was three centimetres away from my nose. To add some excitement I would practice shallow water entries with my 'dive equipment' on. I perfected my shallow water entries by climbing up onto the hand-basin, standing on top of it and jumping into the bath. How I didn't manage to break my neck or legs, I'll never know. Poor Mum or Dad would be left with more water on the floor than in the bath. If the bath wasn't full of water, or Mum and Dad refused to run the bath because of having to mop up all the time, I always had an alternative up my sleeve. Being small and flexible had its advantages. The kitchen and bathroom sinks doubled as a swimming pools and baths!

I started school at Glenfield Primary School in February 1990. My memories of those first few years are very hazy. The only clear memories I have are of one-on-one reading lessons with a teacher aide because my reading level was poor. I also remember sitting on the mat listening to my old and wrinkly teacher reading to the class after lunch. For some reason, perhaps because I wasn't interested in the story, I'd rub my hands on the carpet and lick them clean with my tongue. My mouth watered with the yummy taste. How disgusting is that?!

Six months before I started school, my brother Andrew was born on 13 July 1989. At almost five years old, having a little brother to play with was a real privilege and treat. As we both grew older, we developed a typical brotherly relationship. One moment we'd be best of mates, then the next we'd be teasing each other over the stupidest of things. As predicted by our parents, when we were a bit older we grew out of teasing each other. However, now there is always time for the both of us to harmlessly wind each other up!

Andrew went to the same schools as me. At Westlake Boys High School, it'd be fair to say that Andrew didn't share the same attraction to school that I did. Andrew went to school for four things: physical education, friends, morning tea time and lunchtime – which, just quietly, wasn't actually too far off my own motives for being at school!

At the end of Andrew's fifth form year (year eleven) he decided to leave school to take up an engineering apprenticeship. Now he has no student loan (unlike me), he has money in the bank and he's happy in his work.

Andrew and I are very close, always have been. We go scuba diving, cycling, tramping and partying but I am yet to take him on a mountaineering trip – but it will happen!

In the summer of 1993, when I was eight years old, my parents decided to move house and we ended up moving to a small suburb on the North Shore called Forrest Hill. I was a little startled when I first saw our new house. The back section was like a jungle. It had everything: weta, big fat black rats that ended up in the garage (and then in the rat trap), goldfish in a pond and all the typical birds and insects you'd find in deep dense bush.

After the first week I started to really like it. I'd tear through the bush, play hide-and-seek with my brother and climb trees. The front yard was the size of a small paddock dotted with fruit trees. I made up a few cross country tracks and jumps for my BMX bike. When I wasn't at school I entertained myself for hours on end zooming around the yard on my bike, or tearing through the bush on foot. The only thing I couldn't do at home was go snorkelling – the goldfish pond was too shallow and slimy!

We often went to the beach as a family and every single time, without fail, I'd take my snorkelling gear. As soon as we got to the beach I'd put on my mask and snorkel, slip on my flippers and waddle down to the water's edge like an injured duck. I'd be the first in the water and the last out. The beaches we went to had boring sandy bottoms, no fish, no seaweed, just sand and broken shells. Somehow I'd manage to entertain myself diving up and down, inspecting the sea shells and marvelling at the sand formations created by the motion of the ocean.

Mum, Dad and other family members worked hard on our new house, tidying it up and pulling out trees. Eventually they totally got rid of the beautiful bush on our back section. Mum is a big gardener and Dad always has to be doing something, so they made a great clean-up team. They were forever painting, building, trimming trees and gardening – to this day, they're still like this! Within the space of a year or two, the house and section slowly changed, for the better I suppose. At the time I wasn't too fond of the changes but I slowly got used to them. I couldn't spend days running around in the backyard bush anymore, so I had to find new things to do and I made new friends through school and around the neighbourhood.

I soon became friends with my next-door neighbour, and the neighbour next to him. They both went to my school and we often hung out together. After watching a few Hollywood war movies together we came up with the game 'gun wars'. It was quite simple really, you needed a plastic gun and had to be good at hiding and fast at running. Basically we'd pretend we were commandos in the army and 'shoot' at each other with our invisible bullets.

It was great fun, except when someone was shot and they argued that they hadn't been, saying stuff like 'nah, you missed'. Arguments often arose and we got bored with that game after a year or so. At least we weren't sitting around on the couch playing video games, watching movies and eating junk food all day. We were running about, getting hot and sweaty, and as a result keeping fit.

We soon discovered an obsession that solved the arguing over whether or not someone was shot. The discovery was the pea-shooter, more commonly known as a 'joey gun'. It was a simple invention that one of us probably learnt to make at school (in the playground of course, not in class!). The barrel of a pea-shooter is made from a small piece of plastic piping, or a cardboard cylinder from the inside of a roll of paper towel, or a bit of thin steel piping if you were lucky enough to stumble across it.

Next we borrowed the rubber gloves Mum used for washing the dishes. We cut the fingers off them then taped them to the barrel of the pea-shooter. The middle finger was always the best. It stretched further, resulting in a faster and more powerful shot. The end result was a long cylinder with a rubber-glove finger masking-taped to one end.

Of course, a pea-shooter is not complete without bullets. We carried out a lot of experiments with different bullets. Monkey apples are small, white, berry-like bullets the size of a small marble. The outer layer is soft like a ripe tomato and the centre is a concrete-hard pip. They are the perfect bullet if you want to leave a mess, as the soft outer splatters itself all over the target, followed by a sharp sting delivered by the pip. Another favourite bullet was the small hard seed of the pohutukawa tree. It was the bullet of choice when in season. After a few years of being in the pea-shooter ammunition market, we figured out that if we stockpiled seeds from the pohutukawa tree towards the end of the seed season, we'd have enough to last us until the start of the next season.

The pea-shooter became a real obsession with my mates and I. We practised using them before school, at school (just kidding), after school, in the weekends, and in the holidays.

My two neighbours and I looked forward to the weekends. Either Saturday or Sunday would be tournament day. We'd decide on a location for the tournament at one of our three houses. Points would be awarded for hitting an opponent. We copped a lot of grief from our parents about the one real danger of using pea-shooters – getting shot in the eye! Fair enough too, so we all began to wear eye protection, like old sunglasses and the goggles our dads wore when using their chainsaws or other dangerous machinery. The use of eye protection sparked an interest in body armour to assist in minimising the sting from being hit by a bullet. For the age we were, about nine or ten years old, we really came up with some exceptional ideas. A good one I remember was cutting up soft drink bottles and tying the plastic on with elastic as body armour. The natural curve of the plastic fitted the curvature of our arms and legs, providing great protection from bullets. We experimented with newspaper, magazines and more plastic to invent some chest and back protection. None of it worked as well as our arm and leg protectors. The only half-decent chest and back protectors we could come up with were made by sticking a thick newspaper up the front and back of our shirts, and tucking our T-shirts into out pants to stop the newspaper falling out. It worked all right until we started to sweat. At the end of the day, the newspaper would be soggy and our skin stained with black ink.

As you can imagine, we looked like a bunch of nutters running around with goggles, bits of plastic and bits of newspaper stuffed up our T-shirts, thinking we were tough

ABOUT ME

and almighty commandos. Luckily we weren't worried the slightest bit about what anyone else thought. The main thing was that we were having fun, using our brains to be inventive and not hurting anyone or anything (except ourselves!) in the process.

After a while the thrill of having pea-shooter wars wore off. I moved on to Wairau Intermediate School, met new friends and found new things to do. I remember the first day at intermediate school. I was so scared about everything. I was worried about finding my way around the school, meeting new friends, whose class I would be in and generally losing my way in the new environment. Eventually I found out that it wasn't too bad at all. I made new friends, my class was good and I soon got to learn the new class and school routines.

With my new school came a whole lot of new opportunities – rugby teams, soccer teams, swimming teams, basketball teams, orchestras and loads more. I was a member of the North Shore Swimming Club when I started intermediate and decided all I wanted to do was swim, so I chose not to participate in any other sports. If only I could go back in time! Now I wish I had taken part in every single sports team and cultural or musical group that was possible. Without giving something a go, how do you know if you will like it? How do you know if you will be any good at it? I wish I had given everything a go, even just for a few weeks. I'll never know now if I would have enjoyed those sports or realised my potential. I could have been an All Black, Black Cap or a rock star but because I didn't give them a go, I'll never know.

As easy as it is to say 'give everything a go', sometimes it's not possible. Time, money and the clash of activity timetables are difficult things to juggle. Even if you only give a few things a go, you might surprise yourself with your natural ability or passion for the activity and do really well.

While I was at intermediate school, Grandad took me

to Goat Island for the first time. Near Leigh, just north of Auckland, Goat Island became one of my favourite places for snorkelling. It's a marine reserve so the fish are used to people sharing their home. The blue cod think they own the place but still let you get within centimetres of them with your camera. If you look carefully in big cracks you can see literally hundreds of crayfish in some places. The crayfish are cheeky at Goat Island. Once I saw a crayfish the size of a small dog in a large crevice. It confidently walked sideways out of its little house to greet me then decided I could be a threat and retreated slowly without too much concern. Any other place and the crayfish would have scuttled back into the depths if disturbed in the slightest way.

Between the ages of ten and thirteen, I swam competitively at the North Shore Swimming Club based at the Takapuna Pools. I really enjoyed swim training as I felt I was building a good level of fitness and it boosted my confidence when snorkelling. With good fitness and feeling competent in the water, I could swim far offshore out to the deep water reefs whenever I was out snorkelling. I wouldn't say I was the most competitive swimmer in my swim group but I did train hard. As much as I enjoyed swim training, when race day came about I felt really nervous and sometimes even considered not racing. I probably needed some coaching in how to control my nerves and prepare for race day – I wish I had had that. I moved up a few swimming groups through hard work and determination over the first two years. Towards the end of my last year at intermediate I noticed swimmers in my swim group were getting faster and moving up to the next group. I tried my best, but I remained in the same swim group and started to become a little frustrated and lose interest in swimming. Eventually I lost all interest, just before starting high school.

In February 1998, I started secondary school at Westlake

Boys High School. On my first day, along with hundreds of other third formers (or turd-formers), I was crammed into the hot and stuffy lower gym. I was nervous, just as I had been on my first day at intermediate school. Based on the marks scored in the preliminary examinations for high school we were all divided into thirteen classes or streams. In the first stream were the 'smartest' third formers and the thirteenth stream had the 'least smart' third formers in the whole school. My name was called towards the end of the list for the thirteenth class. An hour later I was sitting in class with all of my thirteenth stream classmates. I was a little shocked with the stream I had ended up in but was relieved when I was told by my teacher that if I worked hard I could move up a stream by getting good marks in the mid-year exams.

There sure were a few rascals in that class and we managed to have some great laughs over the first half of the year. I soon made friends with a guy named Brad Stephens and we've been great mates ever since.

I worked and studied hard in the first half of my third form year (which is the same as year nine now) and surprised myself in the mid-year exams. I was moved up seven whole streams into the sixth stream. I was so happy with myself, and from then on I knew that if I put in the effort, I would get the results.

Around the time I gave up competitive swimming, I heard about a sport called water polo. With my swimming skills I decided I'd give it a go. Water polo is played in a pool with a depth of two metres or more so the players can't touch the bottom. There are thirteen players in a team. Six players play at all times, as well as a goalie. One team wears white caps and the other team wears blue caps. The caps tie up under your chin and have plastic ear guards. The game consists of four quarters, each taking five minutes for juniors and longer for seniors. It is a physically tough and rough game requiring a high level of swimming fitness, as well as strong legs to propel your upper body out of the water. You also need a certain amount of brain to suss out the game's tactics.

A call came through in the daily notices for all those who were new to the school and interested in water polo to meet at interval time. I went to the meeting along with thirty or so other third formers. A week later I was part of the Westlake Junior B team, lined up at the start wall of the pool, not having the faintest idea of the rules or what to do. The whistle blew and I torpedoed off the wall, intending to give it my best shot. I picked the ball up with two hands and the referee instantly turned the ball over to the opposition. I learnt that rule quickly – only pick the ball up with one hand.

In all the games I played in my third form year, I think I only scored two goals, but I enjoyed the sport so much that my water polo career lasted ten years. It was the beginning of lifelong friendships, side-splitting laughs and learning a whole load of life skills. I truly believe the water polo culture shaped me into the person I am today.

I enjoyed water polo more than swimming, mainly because of the team environment. Although competitive swimming is great, swimming is an individual sport and I liked water polo's team atmosphere. My swim training had put me in good shape for water polo and I easily transferred sports. I liked the change from repetitively swimming up and down a pool and there were certainly more laughs to be had in the team environment. Water polo was exciting, and at the end of our ball trainings our coach would get us to do an obstacle course, which involved attempting to walk up hydro slides against the swift flowing water, jumping off the highest diving boards, climbing over bulkheads and underwater challenges. This bit of fun at the end of a session made all the hard work worth it.

In the end-of-year exams I tried hard again, put in the effort and got the results. In fourth form I managed to move up one stream to the fifth stream. I also moved up to the Westlake Junior A water polo team. The team was full of highly skilled up-and-coming New Zealand water polo representatives and we won the Auckland and North Island championships. I was having so much fun, I had made good friends, I thrived on the team environment and was passionate about the game.

One school holidays during fourth form, I went up to Goat Island with three friends I played water polo with, Chris Broome, Ash Blythen and Charles Cornhill (a.k.a. Chaz). At that time, you were allowed to feed the fish in the marine reserve. (You're not allowed to do it now as it disturbs the fish's feeding patterns. The fish begin to rely on humans to feed them whereas they should be hunting out their own food.) Usual fish fodder was frozen peas, any type of bread and meat if you wanted to turn the fish into savage piranhas.

This particular school holidays, we had bread, peas and a special treat – corn. We swam out off the beach and came across a school of hungry-looking snapper, so Ash, Charles and I decided it would be laugh to throw a whole lot of bread, peas and corn at Chris and see what would happen. Well, we got more than we bargained for!

All of a sudden about twenty snapper started rocketing towards Chris and the fish food. One snapper mistook Chris's left nipple for a piece of bread. That sure made him leap out of the water! We were all laughing so hard our masks were filling with water. (Try grinning with a dive mask on and you'll see why.) Blood was seeping into the water from Chris's nipple, so we all made a dash for the shore as the next fish to bite one of us could possibly be a shark!

Once on the beach – all laughing except Chris – we carried

out a closer inspection of Chris's nipple. It was hanging by a few threads of skin and was bleeding a lot. No big deal we thought, stick a plaster on it and he'll be right – and he was. To this day Chris has normal nipples.

Water polo took up so much of my time that I didn't have the chance to get involved in the oodles of other sports offered at high school. I wasn't too fussed as I was so happy with where I was heading with water polo. Each week we would do four one-hour swim training sessions, and two one-and-a-half hour ball sessions. We'd play against other schools on one weeknight and on Saturday or Sunday night every week.

During the weekends, holidays, at school and after school I would hang out with friends I played water polo with. This was important, as we got to know each other outside of training and games and formed tight friendships.

A few of my friends and I decided to go on a mission along the coast near where we lived. At high tide, the sea would come right in to the bottom of the cliffs on the shoreline. If we had attempted to go along the coastline at low tide, there would have been some flattish rocks to walk along and no cliffs impeding our progress. Naturally, the easier it was, the less fun it would be, so we chose high tide to attempt our so-called 'mission'. We estimated it would take us three hours to complete. It took us seven!

Most of the time we were jumping from rock to rock or swimming in waves that were breaking against the cliffs and rocks. A few times we attempted a little rock climbing across a vertical cliff with the ocean one or two metres below us. If we fell, we just hoped there would be no rocks hiding underneath the surface.

The first seven-hour attempt didn't put us off and we kept trying to improve our times. On one occasion we had just finished rock hopping and were attempting some low-key rock climbing when we reached a point that was impossible to pass. One of us had to 'take one for the team' and fall into the water to check for rocks – unfortunately the boys unanimously decided that that person was me.

Luckily I missed any rocks and the water was above head height. I looked up from where I was treading water to see one of my friends, Ash Blythen, perched on a small rock ledge and the others were standing on some rocks a bit behind him. Ash called out to me to say that he needed to take a poo and there was no way he could wait. The others standing on the rocks burst out laughing. I understood Ash's difficult situation and wondered how he would solve his awkward problem. Without warning he launched himself off the ledge into the water next to me.

He was underwater for a second or two. When Ash surfaced he said, 'I'm going right now.'

At first, I didn't get what he meant but slowly it dawned on me.

'What? ... oh, no ... no you're not!'

Out of the depths, just like a submarine surfacing, a gigantic poo surfaced right next to me!

I didn't know whether to laugh or cry. I swam off in a desperate attempt to get as far away from the floating log as possible. To my horror the floater was caught in the eddy of water behind me as I tried to swim away. The log followed me for a few strokes until I found a suitable rocky outcrop to climb up onto and get out of the water.

I tried twice to get out but I kept slipping off the rocks and back into the water. Meanwhile the waves were gently moving the floater closer and closer to me. My friends watched the whole time as I was chased by the poo that seemed to have a mind of its own. They never stopped laughing.

Eventually I climbed up onto the rocks and to safety. The rest of my friends chose a different cluster of rocks to exit the water from to avoid the nasty floater.

Hours later, after more rock climbing, rock hopping and swimming, we reached our destination. We'd had a very interesting day, to say the least, and we went on many more similar missions, without encountering any unusual looking floating logs.

In my fifth form year (year eleven) I was chosen for the Westlake Premier water polo team. Being a part of the Westlake Premier water polo team was the sporting highlight of my school years. I already knew my teammates really well from spending time together outside school and playing water polo together over the last two years. For three years in a row we won the New Zealand secondary school water polo championships. We were unbeatable and were dubbed the 'dream team'.

Apart from having very skilled players who were New Zealand water polo representatives in the team, I believe there were a lot of other ingredients that made us so successful. Our coach, Carl Ainley, was young so we got on well with him. He had good theoretical and practical knowledge of water polo, as well as good sporting ethics. He really knew how to get the best out of our team. He trained us hard and taught us discipline, respect and time management. He made sure everyone got on well as a team and had one common goal: to win. There were rules in place; we respected that and knew the consequences if we broke them. For every minute that we were late to training we had to do ten press ups. I think the most anyone ever did was six hundred. If we missed training without an acceptable reason the punishment was fifteen minutes of butterfly without any rest. When it was game time or training time we were serious, listened carefully and asked questions if we weren't sure. As soon as the serious time was over we'd always have some fun and joke around. We had frequent team get-togethers that galvanised our friendships and helped us function well as a team when in the pool and under pressure.

We always had brilliant parental support. The countless hours parents spent watching our games and driving us around is commendable. A lot of the time, support from parents goes unnoticed, so take the time to thank those who help out – without them sport is impossible. Without the support from our parents, chances are we wouldn't be playing water polo and we certainly wouldn't have been a winning team. Almost everyone's parents came to watch our games and supported us unconditionally. Before we could drive, they'd be up at 5 a.m. to get us to 5.30 a.m. trainings a few mornings a week, as well as driving us a few afternoons a week and for at least one game a week. They paid our outrageously expensive pool fees, tournament fees and tour fees – thanks!

Tours were the highlight of water polo and usually consisted of four or five days out of town. The team, including coaches and managers, were booked into a motel with four or five of us to a room. We'd be left to look after ourselves and do most of our own cooking – with varying degrees of success.

As teenage guys on the loose out of town, you can imagine we'd have an awesome time and get up to some mischief. And we did.

One evening a fire extinguisher 'accidentally' went off and powder coated the entire room, including the carpet, television, couches and dining table. The motel manager was unimpressed and left us with a cleaning bill. I can't recommend this trick to anyone but it sure seemed funny at the time.

Another evening, I was assigned dinner duty. I put a pot of peas on the stove and left it for an hour while I watched television. The fire alarm gave me a heck of a fright, and a terrible smell met me as I rushed into the kitchen. On the stove top, I found the pot with an inch of black charcoal furiously steaming away. No matter how hard I tried I couldn't remove the burnt peas and the pot was ruined. I hid it towards the back of the cupboard and hoped the motel manager didn't find it. The room absolutely stank of smoke until the next morning.

Initiations of junior players were part of the fun, with no malice or harm intended. On a junior's first tour away with the team, they had to undergo several initiations. Outrageous haircuts were part of the tradition. A number-one head shave, a bowl cut, a mullet or a custom design from one of the senior team members ensured juniors were easily identified at all times. The juniors also did most of the cooking and cleaning, as well as looking after the team's water bottles, water polo balls and caps.

Most of my Westlake teammates and I played for the North Sport Water Polo Club as well as for our school team. That meant twice as many games and training sessions but could only help improve our game and fitness. North Sport was the provincial team for our district and brought together the district's top players. Through school I played for the North Sport under-sixteen and under-eighteen teams. Both age-group teams won the national club championships for two years in a row. I left school in 2002 and continued playing for the under-eighteen and under-twenty teams, winning the under-eighteen and under-twenty national club championships in 2002 and 2003, and the under-twenty national club championships in 2003 and 2004.

CHAPTER THREE

INTENDED TONGARIRO TRAVERSE – DAY ONE

When you have gone so far that you can't manage another step, then you've gone just half the distance that you're capable of.
TRADITIONAL PROVERB FROM GREENLAND

For months I had been nagging my friend James to come on a mountaineering trip with me. He had never been mountaineering before and I wanted to show him how amazing it is. I suggested spending about a week in the Tongariro National Park, a World Heritage Area south of Lake Taupo in the North Island. I did some trip planning one night and realised that I had never done a traverse from the south to the north of the Tongariro National Park, or climbed the park's three main peaks – Mt Ruapehu (2797 metres), Mt Ngauruhoe (2287 metres) and Mt Tongariro (1967 metres) – all in one go. The trip I had in mind wouldn't need a high degree of mountaineering skills so it would be ideal for James as a beginner. Although quite long, I thought it would be perfect for him to get a taste of mountaineering.

I called James and explained my exact intentions and the dates that might suit both of us and offered him some of my gear to borrow. I was relieved when James agreed to my plan and we decided we would attempt it in the first week of the third-term school holidays. James and I are both primary school teachers so we'd be on holiday then too. The weeks leading up to the school holidays were pure excitement for both of us.

The first Monday of the school holidays started for me at 5.30 a.m. sharp. That's just how I like it – waking at the crack of dawn. As always before leaving home for an extended adventure, I had a super brekky of two pieces of toast, one can of baked beans, two poached eggs, grated cheese and a healthy sprinkle of pepper. I pile all of that up in a bowl then give it a vigorous mix – now that's a breakfast for adventurers: a good serving of toast for carbohydrates and long-lasting energy, then the baked beans, eggs and cheese for protein to help muscle repair and growth.

I whispered goodbye to Mum and Dad, who were still in bed. Dad was snoring like a chainsaw but Mum was half awake and wearily replied, 'Be careful, have fun and we'll see you next week.'

'Yeah, yeah, I'll be fine. I'll ring when we're out.'

Thankfully Mum doesn't worry if I don't ring when I'm in the bush or mountains. She knows only too well my philosophy: 'no news is good news'. Besides, cell phones hardly ever get reception in New Zealand national parks and out-of-the-way places, so chances are I wouldn't be able to call her anyway. I only take a phone for weather updates and emergencies. However, I *don't* rely on a cell phone as a line to the outside world in an emergency. Reception is *always* an unknown factor. Besides, they're a real pest at times. A ringing phone can ruin the true outdoor experience and that unique feeling of isolation. Imagine a week of no text messages, picture messages, emails or phone calls – oh the peace!

After saying goodbye to Mum I carefully packed my car with all my equipment, paying close attention to be sure nothing was left out: pack in the back seat tightly secured with the seatbelt, sharps (such as ice axes, crampons and snow stakes) in the boot along with other bits and pieces like my boots and helmet, and not forgetting spare clothes for the drive home. I tell a lie, the spare clothes in the boot were actually in case we finished the trip early so we could go and party it up at the Powder Keg in Ohakune, a popular bar and restaurant very close to the mountain.

I was running a tad late as usual but wasn't fussed. I backed down the driveway, and drove up the road looking back at the house through my rear-view mirror. See you in a week, I was thinking. Boy, was I excited...oh yeah! I couldn't help the grin on my face growing ear-to-ear – I was on my way to the mountain. A feeling of excitement grows inside me more and more each time I'm heading into the outdoors for an adventure.

I whizzed down the southern motorway to James's house in my trusty blue Honda Civic. I began the drive listening to U2, one of my favourite bands. I was singing at the top of my lungs, almost lifting the car roof off. Anyone who passed me was likely to think I was a bit loopy – but who cares, I was happy.

Along with practising to be a rock star, I was checking off in my head all the equipment I had packed, just in case I had forgotten something. Every item of equipment and clothing was essential and to forget an item might mean having to return home – not something you'd want to do, as the drive from Auckland to Mt Ruapehu takes about four and a half hours one way!

When I got to James's house I transferred a tonne of mountaineering gear from my car to his. We gave our intentions to James's mum. Trip intentions are so important. The more specific and accurate, the better. A good set of intentions should explain where you are planning to go, any alternative plans in case the original plan doesn't work out, how long you plan to stay at each location, the equipment and clothing you have, any medical information, your experience, and most importantly, what time and date you are due home. All these details are used in an emergency or if you are overdue from a trip. Whenever you go on an adventure, make sure you leave intentions with someone responsible; otherwise if you go missing or get injured you may be waiting a very, very long time until someone notices you're in trouble. Also, if you have been clear about where you intend to be, the search area will be much smaller, making it much easier for the rescue teams to find you.

After leaving detailed intentions with James's mum we jumped into the car and headed north – not south. What a pity! James had forgotten to hand in an important document at university for an assignment. If he didn't hand it in before we went away, chances are he would fail his assignment. I didn't mind the slight delay to the beginning of the trip – I was on holiday and soooo looking forward to six days in the crisp mountain air, free of assignments, cell phones and the hustle and bustle of the city.

The drive south went smoothly – considering James was driving. When James drives there are two speeds: foot flat on the accelerator or on the brake. I was rather sleepy on the drive down since I'd had a late Saturday night and arrived home in the early hours of Sunday morning. I was enjoying a bit of shut-eye when James missed the National Park turn off and went about thirty minutes in the wrong direction towards another of the North Island's well-known mountains: Mt Taranaki! Mt Taranaki is to be found at the westernmost part of the central North Island.

I woke up as we passed through a tunnel. Straight away I knew we were going the wrong way ... oops!

'James, where are we?'

'Ah ... on the way to Ruapehu ...,' James said, acting like I'd asked a stupid question.

INTENDED TONGARIRO TRAVERSE – DAY ONE

'No way, I've never seen that tunnel before!' I uttered in disbelief.

As soon as we found a suitable place to do a U-turn, we headed back the way we came. Because I had been asleep, I was a bit unsure of where we actually were. We backtracked, counting the kilometres, and soon came across some road works. We slowed down and I hung out the window to ask the lollipop man, who was holding a stop–go sign.

'Gidday, mate. Hey, are we on the right way to Mt Ruapehu?'

He confidently answered, 'Yep, keep going until you come across a massive sign with 'National Park' on it.'

I chuckled to myself and asked, 'James, how on earth did you miss the massive sign?!'

'I dunno, I was just driving and following the road,' James explained a bit sheepishly.

Several hours later, with my excitement just a few degrees off boiling point, the beautiful Mt Ruapehu came into view. Whenever I see Mt Ruapehu, it acts like an enormous magnet and my eyes feel like delicate metal filings that get sucked towards it. The closer I get to the mountain, the stronger the magnetic field seems. Driving up State Highway 48 with the luxurious Bayview Chateau Tongariro Hotel in the foreground and magnificent Mt Ruapehu in the background is every photographer's dream.

James slowed down as we passed the Chateau and turned right into the Whakapapa visitors' car park. James backed the car into a parking space in front of the toilet block and stopped with the back of the car under the cover of the extended roof. That way we were under cover and could use some nearby seats to pile our large amount of equipment onto. We attached spades, crampons, ice axes, pee bottles and more onto our packs and got geared up ready to go. My ice axe and crampons are special and important tools of the trade for mountaineering. Like a builder has his hammer and nails, I have my ice axe and crampons.

I love getting into my thermals, overpants, and jacket. I feel safe and prepared to deal with the harsh elements. Once I had all that on I brushed my feet with my hands, being sure to remove anything that shouldn't be there, and then I put my socks on. I'm extremely fussy with my feet, socks and boots. And so I should be, because my feet need to be in top condition for walking. When out in the wilderness, I can be on my feet for up to twelve or more hours a day. Sore feet with blisters are ghastly. First, I put thin thermal socks on my feet, followed by thick mountaineering socks, being sure not to leave a single crease in the fabric. I slid my feet into my boots and tied them up firmly – ready to go!

James locked the car and stashed his keys in the top pocket of his pack. We both hauled our heavy packs onto our backs. They weighed about twenty-five to thirty kilograms each. Why so heavy? Well, six days worth of food takes up just as much room, if not more room, than the rest of the equipment in a pack. I always take the same food because I know I get a sufficient amount of energy from it, it's easy to cook, tastes good and isn't too expensive.

For breakfast I have cereal with lots of nuts, fruit and flakes. I use powdered milk to make hot milk to pour over my cereal – yum! Lunch is made up of crackers, the hard kind that taste a bit like cardboard – they're great as they don't get easily crushed in my pack. On the crackers I put Marmite, salami and cheese. Salami has a lot of fat in it and gives you more energy than you get from the carbohydrates in the crackers. Dinner is my favourite meal: dehydrated pasta with the powdered flavouring pre-mixed into the packet. It's effortless to cook, you just add water and bring it to a boil. A sachet of tuna goes down a treat when mixed into the pasta.

With the huge amount of energy used up by walking and

INTENDED TONGARIRO TRAVERSE – DAY ONE

climbing, I wouldn't be able to finish the day without regular snacks. Snacks are super important. I find the best snack is scroggin, which is a mixture of dried fruit, lots of chocolate and nuts. High energy bars also keep the hunger at rest and the body performing like a V8 running on jet fuel.

Liquids are essential too, but it's impossible to carry a day's worth of water. The mountain air is dry and causes dehydration quicker than at sea level. Up there I tend to drink at least four litres of water per day! Fortunately, up in the mountains, I'm surrounded by water all the time. In good weather it's possible to melt snow or ice with a cooker then make a hot cup of tea to rehydrate.

The challenge of fitting six days worth of food into both of our packs seems minor when compared with packing a full kit of mountaineering equipment. My pack is specially designed to be lightweight and durable, and it's fitted with many gear loops, holds and ties. When packing my pack, I keep in mind how I will unpack it, therefore putting the items that I need frequently, like my drink bottle and gloves, at the top. Items that I don't need during the day are further down, towards the bottom. At the very bottom is my sleeping bag, which is made from warmth-giving goose down. Warm air is trapped by the down feathers, keeping me warm and keeping the cold air out. The outer fabric of my sleeping bag is water resistant and keeps out any melting snow.

On top of my sleeping bag is my spare clothing: one pair of merino wool underwear, one long-sleeved thermal and one long-legged pair of thermals, both made from polypropylene. Two pairs of socks are purposely stuffed into areas or gaps of wasted space. It's important that every spare bit of space is filled with something, otherwise you won't be able to carry as much equipment and food as possible.

My down jacket is super warm, made the same way as my sleeping bag. It's perfect for wearing at night and on bitterly cold mornings. Stacked neatly next to my down jacket are my cooking pots and mug. I've never liked washing dishes, and by eating out of the cooking pot I save having to carry the extra weight of a plate. You might think that worrying about a 200 gram plate is a little over the top but everything adds up and counting the grams makes a big difference over six long and tiring days.

To save even more space, I fill my cooking pots with small items of food. Making the most of space in your pack is so important, you'll be surprised how much more you can fit into a well thought out and carefully packed pack.

To cook meals and melt water I use a very lightweight titanium cooker that burns white spirit. White spirit is a type of fuel, like LPG or petrol, except it burns hotter and has a much lower freezing point, meaning it won't freeze in sub-zero conditions. At 0°C and colder, the white spirit will still remain liquid and burn very hot, as opposed to LPG which would freeze and not work. My cooker sits next to my cooking pots.

Next I pack all the food, except a few muesli bars that I put in my top pocket for easy access. A very important piece of equipment that I place quite close to the top of my bag is my first aid kit.

The type of weather determines whether I pack or wear my insulating and protective clothing. If it's cold and windy, I'll wear my overpants, jacket and insulating polar fleece jacket. Fine weather is great but it means having to put protective clothing in your pack, making it a bit heavier.

Small items such as a knife, toothbrush, sunscreen, lip balm and drink bottle are kept in a resealable plastic bag in the top pocket of my pack. I don't take toothpaste in order to save weight (and someone else always takes some!).

On the outside of my pack, attached with loops, holds and ties, is my essential mountaineering equipment. As you read on you'll begin to notice that with a little Kiwi ingenuity just about every piece of mountaineering equipment has multiple uses.

When the snow is soft, not requiring crampons, elastic ties fasten my crampons to my pack. Those same elastic ties can be used to secure anything from a drink bottle to gloves or a jacket. If walking on flat terrain and soft snow I use my walking sticks. Walking sticks aren't for grandads or grannies, they genuinely help your balance and take the pressure off your knees when descending a steep slope. They also help you keep a good posture and straight back. Once the terrain gets steeper or it becomes necessary to use an ice axe, I remove my ice axe from the ice axe loop on my pack and put my walking stick in its place. When not climbing steep snow or ice, my second ice axe is fastened next to my crampons in a second ice axe loop. The second axe has a hammer on it for banging in snow stakes, which are also fastened to the side of my pack.

Snow stakes are used as an anchor or protection to stop a fall on steep hard snow. Without a rope you cannot use snow stakes for climbing, so we were going to use them as stormproof tent pegs for firmly holding the tent in place in windy conditions. Slings – not the kind you use for a broken arm – are similar in shape to a rubber band, except not stretchy and usually with a length of at least one and a half metres. They come in various sizes and are mainly used for protection and are attached to snow stakes when climbing with a rope. An alternative use is attaching a sling to a snow stake, so it acts as an extender when pitching a tent. A third use, which I find very handy, is to wrap a sling around your upper body from one shoulder to the opposite hip. Then with a carabiner, which also has unlimited uses, you can attach your ice axe leash to the sling around your upper body. This will act as a safeguard if you drop your ice axe.

A lightweight shovel made from aluminium and plastic fits through a conveniently placed carry loop, allowing the shovel to sit nicely down the outside centre of my pack. A shovel has many uses: digging snow caves, building walls around a tent in windy conditions and digging out someone who has been buried by an avalanche.

Another use for a spade – not recommended by the manufacturers – is spade sliding. A shovel provides a super quick means of descending down steep snow slopes, or icy slopes if you're prepared for a nasty wipe-out, bruises and possibly some small cuts. By sitting on the spade head with the shaft and handle between your legs, you can easily, but dangerously, cover vast distances downhill – a cheap thrill, highly recommended, though only if you have a helmet. A brain bucket, more commonly known as a helmet, protects the head from falls, spade sliding and falling rocks and ice – all common occurrences when mountaineering.

Due to the isolated nature of climbing and the often lengthy wait for experienced medical assistance, the only time I take my helmet off is when I go to sleep. It goes on again as soon as I leave my sleeping bag.

Our huge pile of mountaineering equipment wouldn't be complete without a tent and a sleeping mat. When tenting, there's barely enough room for sleeping so our packs must stay outside and withstand the elements. The super lightweight tent weighs in at 2.8 kilograms. It can withstand huge gusts of wind and extreme temperatures, and it has superior ventilation to prevent condensation, and a fairly hefty price tag. This must be the only piece of equipment that only has one effective use – to provide shelter.

A sleeping mat, on the other hand, is a critical piece of equipment with various uses. The obvious one being for sleeping on. Its construction of closed-cell foam prevents cold air travelling through to the sleeping bag, and eventually to

INTENDED TONGARIRO TRAVERSE – DAY ONE

the sleeping person. The foam is very lightweight and cheap, and a puncture from an ice axe or crampon won't compromise it in any way. Rolled up, sleeping mats also make great leg splints for broken legs. An injured person can be dragged through the snow on one too. Something not recommended by the manufacturer (but recommended by me) is using one as a toboggan in soft snow – another cheap thrill!

The preparation and inspection of equipment, getting the right gear on and putting on a pack must feel similar to what soldiers go through as they prepare for combat. Some of the emotions must be similar too: apprehension, fear and excitement.

After gearing up in the car park at Whakapapa village, we still had two more important things to do before we left the car park. That was to leave our intentions with the Department of Conservation (DOC), and organise a lift up to the end of the road where the ski field begins, also known as the Top of the Bruce.

As I said before, intentions are so important. Getting used to the weight of our packs, we waddled across the road to DOC at the Whakapapa visitors centre. I filled in the pink intentions form while James checked out the weather. I wrote a very detailed summary of where we would be staying, the equipment we had and our emergency contact details. I discussed the weather at length with James and was happy with the forecast. With help from DOC we managed to organise a lift to the Top of the Bruce. We waited outside for some kind of four-wheel drive or bus to arrive. To our surprise, a white wagon, looking similar to a rusty bucket, coughed and spluttered to a stop. I was thinking, Gee, I really hope this piece of junk manages to get us up the mountain road.

Out stepped a man with dreadlocks down to his shoulder blades, who casually asked, 'William Pike and James Christie?'

'Yes, that's us,' I replied.

We dumped our bags in the boot, and I got in the front seat, James in the back. The man got into the car and introduced himself. He turned the key and nothing happened. The car wouldn't start!

Great start, I thought to myself a bit sarcastically.

'No worries guys, this always happens,' he said, sounding full of confidence.

'OK,' I politely replied.

The guy got out, fiddled with something under the bonnet, got back in the car and turned the key. The car coughed into life and we were on our way at last. To our surprise, the rusty wreck made it to the Top of the Bruce without further incident. We climbed out, thanked our trusty driver and grabbed all our gear.

At approximately 4 p.m., James and I both set foot in the snow. It was all on now, the fun, excitement and apprehension. Woohoo!!! We plodded up the ski field in pleasant weather, getting used to the weight of our packs and making adjustments with straps here and there. I noticed the snow cover was thin; there was a lot less snow than a few weeks ago. We quickly agreed to make a decision on tenting or snow caving once we arrived at our proposed camp or cave site.

I showed James the basics of using an ice axe: always holding it in the uphill hand ready to self arrest. Self arrest is a funny term. It means to use an ice axe to stop yourself sliding on steep snow or ice. If you can imagine tripping over on a sixty-degree slope and sliding on concrete-hard snow towards a hundred-metre cliff, you will understand the importance of being able to self arrest quickly and efficiently.

In between our conversations on what form of shelter we should sleep in and where, we talked about how and why avalanches happen.

Avalanches give me the willies – 'white death', some

INTENDED TONGARIRO TRAVERSE – DAY ONE

people call them. I've read lots of books explaining how avalanches happen, where they are most likely to happen and how to rescue someone buried by an avalanche. Still, I didn't feel totally comfortable in predicting possible avalanches and felt like I could learn some more. Without putting James off, I basically explained that the weather plays a large part in reducing or maximising avalanche danger. Wind, temperature, rain, sun and unstable weather patterns are all responsible for raising the possibility of an avalanche. For instance, strong wind can easily move snow and deposit it on the leeward side of the slope, and too much fresh snow on a steep slope can be unstable and cause an avalanche.

After an hour and a half of walking, the Ruapehu Hut came into sight. As we got closer, we veered to the right in search of the snow caves dug a few weeks beforehand by members of the New Zealand Alpine Club (NZAC), who were on a training course.

Looking down from high above the snow cave site, I could see at least twenty people. I said to James, 'The snow cave option doesn't look too promising, with all those people I'd say it'll be a full house. I'd rather snow cave than pitch our tent, though.' We continued walking through soft snow, past a few people, to a vague imperfection in the snow, which looked like a snow cave entrance.

Something caught my eye in the distance distracting me from the snow caves. When I turned back to look at the possible snow cave entrance, I saw a face with a smile on it was poking out, welcoming us in. I couldn't make out the face because of a balaclava, snow goggles and a helmet, but a woman's voice called out, 'Hi there, how you going?'

'Great,' we replied together.

'How much room do you have in there?' I questioned, trying not to sound rude and worrying about cramping their style.

'Oh, there's plenty of room for the both of you, come on in. Would you like a cup of something hot?'

I must say that everyone in the outdoors is ten times nicer and more accommodating than people can be in the city. I mean, it's not every day you can rock up to a stranger's place, they invite you in – having never met you before – and then they offer you a cup of something hot! I just wish everyone was that nice back in the city, what a difference it would make.

Crawling on my hands and knees through the snow cave entrance with a smile on my face, I said, 'A cup of tea, no milk will be great thanks.' James was right behind me and politely asked for a tea, with milk.

With helmets and snow goggles off I realised that there was also a man in the snow cave. It looked rather roomy and well laid out.

A snow cave is built by digging into the side of a snow slope with a shovel. A heat trap is made by making the floor higher than the entrance – remember heat rises. This can be achieved by digging inwards, then upwards, and then shaping the inside of the snow cave to your desired dimensions. The ceiling needs to be smooth to prevent any drips, and a hole – created by an ice axe shaft – in the roof helps the air to circulate.

I sat next to James on the cold snow, still fully geared up except for my helmet and snow goggles. After a few minutes of chatting to the man and woman I found out that they were both instructors from the Sir Edmund Hillary Outdoor Pursuit Centre (OPC), which is based in Turangi, near Taupo. OPC offers all sorts of adventure-based programmes. I've been on two of their programmes and they totally rock.

The snow cave next door to us had twenty high-school kids bouncing off the walls. From memory, they were prefects on an adventure week. Luckily snow caves are like soundproof rooms. When a storm is raging or kids are making a racket next door to you, you can't hear a thing and you always have the best night's sleep ever! Surprisingly snow caves are also warm – warmer than a tent. You can lean against the walls and make your own personalised shelves for equipment; an awesome experience if you ever get the chance!

Before we made dinner I decided to prepare the snow cave for bedtime. Our packs were still outside and it was going to be difficult to drag them past the two OPC instructors. The solution was simple. I'd get my spade and dig from outside of the snow cave, directly into where we would be sleeping. James helped too, and soon I was peering into our white soon-to-be bedroom. I crawled through the small hole we'd created. Then I smoothed the roof over to stop any drips caused by our body heat and flattened the floor to make it comfortable to sleep on. There's nothing worse than sleeping on an uneven ground. There was plenty of room in the cave. It was so wicked! We dragged our gear inside and I couldn't wait to get into my sleeping bag and marvel at the beauty of being in a snow cave.

I dug out some pasta from my pack and, to my surprise, the two instructors offered us some of their dinner. They said they had heaps left over; heaps of beautiful big burritos. They *did* have a lot left over but not after James and I got our hands on it. The burritos where huge, filled with hot mince with a yummy sauce, carrots and loads of cheese. I can't think of a nicer dinner that I've had in the outdoors. Better still, we didn't have to cook, or do any dishes. I did offer to do the dishes – my mum will be surprised at that! The only downside to not eating our own dinner was the fact that we would have the same amount of weight in our packs when walking tomorrow!

Our snow cave was a five-minute walk from the Ruapehu Hut (operated by the NZAC), across a tidy looking ski run and up a fifty-degree slope. To get up the slope, you needed to use an ice axe and crampons because of the icy surface.

As quickly as I ate the burritos, they needed to come out again. With James, I wandered up to the Ruapehu Hut to use their loos. It beats leaving a brown mess and a yellow snow cone for some poor skier to slide over on and stain his or her latest and greatest ski wear. It also has a pretty negative effect on the environment.

Looking east from the Ruapehu Hut entrance, you look directly at Pinnacle Ridge, which offers sublime mountaineering and climbing and has a series of three unrelenting razor sharp peaks that look like something out of the movie *Touching the Void*. The Ruapehu Hut was like five-star accommodation compared to our barren and frozen cave. Electricity, foam mattresses, microwaves, two flush toilets, heaters and a drying room are all part of the package in the Ruapehu Hut – but no shower, sorry.

Most likely you are wondering why on earth we would choose to sleep in a snow cave instead of a comfy, warm, spacious hut with up-to-date technology. Simple really: the hut was booked out. But that's not the only reason – it's quieter in a snow cave. It's private (though that doesn't mean you can lounge around in the nude) and you can build a snow cave almost anywhere and to your desired dimensions.

As I approached the hut door, I could see light rays from inside the Ruapehu Hut escaping out the windows and creating an unnatural glow on the surrounding snow and ice-covered ground.

Walking into the Ruapehu Hut is like walking into a stranger's house – you never know who you are going to meet. To my surprise, the hut was full of faces I knew well, and it was as much of a surprise for the crowd in the hut. About thirty friends from teachers' college on a physical education outdoor education course had taken over the hut and were casually mooching about chatting, sleeping, cooking and eating.

After using the toilet, I stayed and chatted, explaining our intentions and where we were sleeping. You should have seen some of the girls cringe when I explained to them our style of accommodation – they were horrified at the thought of us sleeping in a snow cave. They had planned to spend a week in the hut while learning basic mountaineering skills as part of their outdoor education course. I mentioned to them that James and I might see them the next day if they walked up to the crater lake.

I had to cut the conversation short, as I was quickly overheating with my layers of warm clothing on – my attire was not really appropriate for a warm hut where everyone else was in T-shirts, shorts and jandals! I was also thinking about sleep; I couldn't wait to head back to our little frozen sanctuary for a quiet night's sleep.

CHAPTER FOUR

OUTDOOR ACTION

The outdoors is a powerful tool in terms of people sorting out where they are at, in terms of confidence. There are no masks. On a mountain or a rock face, you can't hide the fact that you are scared. You can't pretend. In a very short time you can have some intense learning and life-changing situations which would take a long time and a lot of talking to achieve in a classroom. It might never happen at all in a classroom.
BEV SMITH – SIR EDMUND HILLARY OUTDOOR PURSUIT CENTRE INSTRUCTOR 1984–1989

Ever since third form (year nine) I had been hearing rumours about a subject you could take in sixth form (year twelve) that was based solely on outdoor activities. Some of my friends believed it was true, others thought it was a myth. Eager to find the truth, I did some research and found out that it was true. The subject was called outdoor education.

'Forget desks, chairs, books, pens and pencils,' I was told by a senior student who had completed the subject. 'Think tramping, snorkelling, shooting – with real guns – rock climbing and kayaking. *All* during school time,' he added with a grin on his unshaven face. It almost sounded too good to be true, except it *was* true.

At the end of each year, I was slow to submit my subject preference list for the next year. At the end of fifth form (year eleven), I was asking my teacher when I could submit my subject preference list before it was even available. The day my teacher handed me the form I filled it out on the spot and handed it back in. There was no way I was going to miss out on doing outdoor education.

Snorkelling kicked off the first term of outdoor education. We had lots of interesting theory lessons in the classroom on the different types of masks, fins, snorkels, wetsuits, weight belts, knives and locations for snorkelling. At first it seemed odd that we were learning about snorkelling – it was something that I loved so much and never once had any teacher ever taught me about snorkelling. It wasn't like a normal class where someone would always be talking or mucking around. In outdoor education everyone listened, everyone did the set work and everyone was interested.

For the first time ever, I began to see small connections with other mainstream subjects. Maths for example; I'd always thought that I wouldn't use it once I left school, apart from for basic calculations. Our outdoor education teacher, Mr Mullins, began explaining the addition, subtraction and division skills needed for using scuba diving tables to work out crucial decompression information. I began to see the use in learning my times tables when I was asked to convert feet into metres, and metres into atmospheres.

Mr Mullins explained the effects of pressure caused by the water's weight at significant depth. A basic understanding of physics was needed to understand and explain the effects that pressure at depth had on equipment and the human body. I learnt that without a basic understanding of maths and science, I could potentially put myself in danger. From then on I paid a lot more attention in maths and science and always listened out for ways to help me understand the maths and science involved in snorkelling and scuba diving. Becoming a scuba diver was one of my main goals and if I couldn't use my dive tables or understand simple science, I'd be up the creek without a paddle!

In term two the outdoor education focus changed from snorkelling to bushcraft. I was just as excited about bush walking as I had been about snorkelling. We started off learning about the essential clothing and equipment needed for overnight trips in the bush. That also prepared us to beg, borrow or buy the equipment and clothing needed for our end-of-term trip to the Kaimanawa Ranges. We learnt about the absolute necessity of caring for the environment, places to go bush walking (or tramping) and the basics of cooking with outdoor cookers, which is not as easy as you might think.

Map and compass skills were the most difficult to pick up. I remember being lost – not literally, but in class – not having any idea how to use my compass. Once again, maths knowledge was necessary – I was beginning to feel relieved that I had been listening carefully to what my maths teacher had to say lately.

The highlight of bushcraft was the long-awaited trip to the Kaimanawa Ranges for a week. The Kaimanawa Ranges are located to the south-east of Lake Taupo in the North Island. The ranges consist of vast and rugged expanses of native forest, scrubland and tussock in the alpine areas. Common activities that people undertake in the ranges are tramping, fly-fishing, hunting and basic mountaineering during mid-winter.

Monday started off with a five-hour drive. We then did a bush walk that was of a similar length to the drive, eventually pitching our tents in a nice flat spot, near a crystal-clear river. Tuesday we were up bright and early, spending the day learning how to use our maps and compasses for real. Wednesday was a big bush walk with some amazing views along the way. On Thursday, the greatest thrill of all for me had to be learning how to build bivouacs then sleeping in them on survival night. The idea of the survival night is to simulate being lost in the bush with only day-tramping equipment. We weren't allowed a tent, sleeping bag or any overnight equipment. The only equipment we were allowed was what we would have taken if we'd been going on a day walk. This included clothing, footwear, a drink bottle, some small snacks and a survival kit. The kit was very important as it contained life-saving items like matches, a survival blanket, fishing hook and line, pen and pencil and basic first aid requirements.

The survival night began with Mr Mullins letting us choose a partner to spend the night with in the bush. My friend Blake Bouge and I partnered up together. I was happy to be with Blake; I knew him well because we went to primary school together. Blake was in a different form class but for maths he came to my class. I remember we used to sit in the corner of the class, hidden from our teacher's view, sometimes gazing out the window together but always talking about boy stuff. Topics of conversation included building forts in the bush at lunchtime, which girls had cooties and what we wanted to do in the weekend – nothing that related one bit to what we were meant to be learning.

The survival night began. Blake and I pulled on every item of clothing we had and filled our jacket pockets with snacks, a survival kit, a torch and pocket knives. We then happily trotted off along a windy track heading north from our main camp site. We were both bubbling with excitement.

After at least ten minutes, we left the track and started scrambling up a steep bank, which supported humungous trees. We sweated like pigs because of the layers upon layers of clothing we had on. As I came to the top of the steep bank, Blake was close behind me. Although the area was difficult to make out because of the thick undergrowth, the land flattened out to the size of a rugby field. This looks like an all right spot I thought to myself.

'What do you reckon mate?' I asked Blake.

Slightly out of breath and talking through his jacket as he pulled it over his head, Blake mumbled, 'I dunno, let's check it out.' So we did.

As we searched for a suitable area to build our bivouac, splintered beams of sunlight scattered through the giant trees. In the fading minutes of daylight, we came across a gigantic fallen tree with a barren piece of dirt the size of a couple of king size beds to its left. It provided an ideal spot for leaning dead branches and ferns against the tree to form an overhead shelter. Large dead branches made a nice sturdy frame for insulation – piled up ferns and scrub trap heat – and weather proofing. By pointing ferns downwards, like they naturally hang on fern trees, water runs down the fern and off the end, instead of through the bivouac and onto the poor person inside!

The base of the bivouac is the most important part, as you lose so much heat by sitting or lying directly on the ground. In damp areas with low light you can find masses of moist, light green, fluffy moss that easily pulls off whatever it's growing on. By piling up the moss we almost had ourselves a luxurious airbed for the night, as the spongy moss traps warm air. It was looking so comfortable I began to feel sleepy! But it wasn't time for sleep just yet, the next job was to prepare a base for the fire and collect enough firewood to last through the night.

I whizzed off in search of as much dry wood as possible: small twigs, bigger twigs, small branches, bigger branches and lastly the biggest bits of tree I could find – all dead of course. It's important to be careful not to harm any living plants or trees.

When Blake finished preparing a dry flat area to set the

fire on, he gave a loud wolf whistle that I'm sure woke all the animals near us.

Then he yelled, 'Pikey, the base is finished, bring me wood!'

I staggered back to the bivouac with a massive collection of firewood bundled up under both arms and dropped everything near our fireplace.

'Here we go, Blake, your turn now – go get me some wood please, and don't get lost!'

I was confident Blake would not get lost, but with the fading light every tree, fern and bit of bush starts to blend into one, making it easy to get disoriented.

I used my trusty Victorinox pocket knife to slice thin slivers of wood into a pile on top of a small candle from my survival kit. Then using some small twigs and a few bigger twigs, I formed the shape of a pyramid. I struck a match and went to light the candle but the match went out. Damn it! Luckily I had a few extra matches and the candle lit on my second attempt. Immediately the wood began to catch light and the fire was alive!

Fire in the outdoors has something magic about it. You can sit and watch the flickering flames and burnt orange embers for hours and hours. The fire lures you to it, acting like a centrepiece you can sit or lie around in comfort, chatting about anything in the world. You can cook with fire, dry your clothes and keep really warm.

I sometimes think fire is alive, a living organism. Think about it. Here's a small science lesson for you. Scientists classify something as a living organism with the mnemonic MRS GREN, which stands for **M**ovement, **R**espiration (breathing), **S**ensitivity (touch, smell, taste, sight, hearing), **G**rowth, **R**eproduction (producing young/babies), **E**xcretion (poos and wees) and **N**utrition or food. So fire, well, is it living? It could be. Fire moves, it breathes oxygen, it's sensitive to water and air, it reproduces or makes more of itself, it excretes carbon dioxide (a poisonous, colourless and odourless gas) and it 'eats' whatever it's burning. Compare fire with yourself: you move, you breathe, you have senses, you are growing, you can reproduce, you go poos and wees (more smelly than a fire's), and you eat – some of you eat a lot I bet! Interesting isn't it, but scientifically fire is not a living organism, though sometimes it seems it. Anyway, enough of the science lesson and back to the bush.

From the bottom of my lungs I bellowed, 'Bllaakkeee... we have fire... woohooo.'

It was an awesome feeling getting a real fire going, knowing it was going to be used for a real reason – to keep us warm and alive! As I was feeding the fire with more twigs, Blake appeared in front of me with as much firewood as he could possibly carry. Just as well, because Mr Mullins always said that you can never have too much firewood. The tidy Kiwi campers that we are, we neatly sorted all our firewood into piles according to size, putting it around the fire to dry it out.

By the time our fire was loaded with wood and burning well, it was completely dark, and all our surroundings, including ourselves, were bathed in a bright orange glow. It was awesome – just Blake, me, the fire, the bush and not a worry in the world. I was in my element and from then on I knew this was the life for me.

We sat comfortably on our survival blankets and leant against them with our backs. A great thing about survival blankets is their ability to reflect your body's heat back to itself. They are paper thin and look like large sheets of tinfoil. The smallest movement of a survival blanket sounds like a large sheet of tinfoil might do when beating itself to death in a wild gale. Still, they are an essential part of a tramping first aid kit – they save lives! We sat close to the fire, warming our boots and feeling the drying heat on our faces.

With a mouth full of chocolate muesli bar and staring into the flickering flames, I began to tell Blake how I felt like a real caveman, a hunter and gatherer, as though we were living off the land. Instead of eating muesli bars, we should have hunted down huhu grubs and baked them on the fire. Mmmm, a source of protein that tastes just like peanut butter! Try one sometime, I highly recommend it – it will put some hair on your chest.

We chatted on for another hour or two, mostly about how we were enjoying the school trip so far and how cool it was to be in the bush, instead of at school. We piled up more wood on the fire and dozed off to sleep. I knew I'd have to wake a few times during the night to keep the fire going.

Within two hours the fire was down to glowing red embers, in desperate need of wood to keep it going. Blake was asleep and I managed to reach some dry wood to pile onto the embers. It was very cold and I was beginning to shiver until the wood slowly smouldered back to life, back to those lovely warm flames. I didn't expect to find a disaster unfolding the next time I woke up.

I woke with the smell of rubber filling my nostrils. Out of nowhere Blake began freaking out like a cat being squirted by a hose. I looked at the fire and was shocked to see Blake's boot was alight! Now I could see why Blake was freaking. Blake leapt up over the fire and took off at full speed into the pitch black. All I could see was this flaming fireball bouncing up and down off the ground. I didn't know whether to laugh or not. Eventually Blake staggered back holding his melted right boot in his left hand.

Terribly worried, I shouted, 'Blake! Are you OK? Are you burnt?'

He spluttered back, 'Jeez! Um, ah, no I don't think so. My flaming boot was on fire!'

'I know that! Give me a look at your foot.'

My heart was thudding in my chest.

Under torchlight we gave his foot a full inspection, and luckily for Blake it wasn't burnt. The sole of the boot was hanging off like melted cheese and the worst thing was that he had hired the boots!

After the boot stopped steaming Blake managed to put it back on. Much to Blake's disgust, I started to see the funny side of our near-emergency. The sight of him tearing through the bush with his boot on fire made me laugh over and over again.

I was still failing to contain my small outburst of laughter when we settled back down onto our moss bed, covered with our noisy survival blanket sheet. After a while of dozing and being sure *my* boots weren't too close to the fire, I drifted off to sleep.

I awoke to slivers of light being strained though the thick undergrowth. The sun's warmth enhanced the pure sweet smell of the bush – it was a glorious way to begin the day. Blake had woken without me noticing. I'm sure he secretly checked that he still had two boots and two feet. Our fire had completely burnt down to ashes. Blake and I emptied a few litres of water over the ashes to be totally sure there was no chance of it relighting.

We didn't muck around; as soon we had dismantled our bivouac and packed up everything that didn't belong in the bush, we headed for the main camp – we were starving. Making my way back down the steep hill was entertaining. It was so steep, we were able to jump and slide, jump and slide; kind of like skiing all the way down to the track.

Back at camp, Blake and I swapped stories with the other boys about the night just gone, over a hot bowl of undercooked porridge – it tasted great. Blake's mishap took the prize for the most exciting.

Friday was a long, but fun, walk back to the school vans. Blake's boots somehow stayed in one piece over the rugged terrain. The drive home seemed as though it was never going to end – the stench of boys who hadn't showered for five days sent everybody into a light doze until we got back to school.

It was a fantastic trip that made me fall even more in love with the outdoors. I had so much fun and learnt so much about surviving in the bush. It made me beg for more. It was contagious. (Don't tell anyone – but Blake was a bit naughty and returned his hire boots without the shop assistant noticing that they had been crisped in the fire. I hope the next person checked them before they went tramping!)

Midway through sixth form (year twelve), I decided that I wanted a job – not a boring job, but something exciting and different from the ordinary 'schoolboy' job. Working at a supermarket definitely wasn't for me. I needed a little more action than aimlessly swiping items over a barcode scanner for hours on end.

One day when I was at the Dive Centre, a local dive training business, doing a bit of research into learning to dive, I decided it would be cool to work doing something that I love. My number-one passion then was the ocean, so it seemed like a good idea to ask for a job at the Dive Centre.

Before I left the shop with brochures on dive course information, I somehow gathered up the courage to ask for the manager. I asked the manager if he needed anyone to do some part-time work. We talked for a couple of minutes and he said, 'Book yourself onto a dive course and come back and see me.'

Four hundred dollars (40 lawn cuts for my grandparents at $10 each) and a few months later I was booked onto an open-water scuba diving course. The dive course was grand.

I had so much fun and was blown away by the beauty of the underwater environment. I was hooked and couldn't wait to get out diving by myself. I had done a lot of reading and talking to others about great dive sites, and had written a list of around fifteen dive sites that I wanted to dive. Just writing the list was exciting, so ticking each dive site off was unimaginably exhilarating.

Once I'd completed the course, I took a ride on my bike after school to the Dive Centre and chatted to the manager again. He said he needed someone to fill dive cylinders and do some cleaning. The job was mine! I was over the moon and quietly proud of myself. I had won a job that was different from what everyone else was doing.

I worked Mondays after school from 3.30 p.m. to 6 p.m. and all day on Saturdays. I started on $8 an hour, which wasn't too bad compared with what my friends earned working ordinary jobs. When I didn't need a vehicle to carry dive cylinders, I'd ride my bike. I literally lived up the road; it was all downhill, cheap, quick and fun. I could get to work from my house quicker by bike than by car.

Like anything new, it took me a while to get familiar with the job, especially learning how to use the air compressor to fill the dive cylinders. The cleaning was easy and boring; I didn't like that too much. But hey, you can't expect to have all the nice jobs at the beginning. I was a schoolboy, and like most schoolboys in their first job had to do the boring stuff to begin with. Only with experience and hard work do you move up the ranks to bigger and better things. That's the way it goes out in the big wide world of work, so be prepared to start on a small wage, do the average jobs that only *you* seemed to be asked to do. Work hard, prove yourself and then you should expect to see some reward.

Filling dive cylinders sometimes felt like blowing up a balloon in a thorn bush. Dive cylinders are filled while submerged in water in what's called a fill bath. The chances of a dive cylinder actually bursting are extremely small but we still had to be careful. I always felt safe, as the fill bath was made from one-centimetre-thick steel. At just over a metre high, with a capacity of about 200 litres, the fill bath held four dive cylinders. The cylinders floated when empty and sunk once they were full. Yep, all that air weighs a bit!

The valve face of a dive cylinder has a small black O-ring, about the size of a ten cent coin, to seal the connection between the valve face and regulators that you breathe with underwater. A similar connection is used for filling the dive cylinders. Things really get pear-shaped when the little O-ring blows to bits, or slips out under 3300 pounds per square inch (psi) of pressure. Reasons for the O-ring blowing are, one: it is old and needs replacing; two: it wasn't fitted correctly in the first place; and three: pure bad luck. Car tyres have about thirty pounds per square inch of pressure in them, and when an O-ring blows at 3300 psi it doesn't leave too much water in the fill bath.

When an O-ring blows, there is usually no warning and I've nearly had to change my underwear numerous times. Every customer in the shop nearly jumped out of their skin when an O-ring blew.

Whenever it happened, my heart instantly began to beat at twice its maximum rate. Air screams from the valve face in all directions, effortlessly replacing the surrounding water with air. Air travelling quickly at high pressure freezes, so I had to be aware of tiny icicles travelling out from the valve face at the speed of a bullet. They were not to be avoided by ducking and running for cover, but by staying put and turning the handle off to stop the air flowing out. Water from inside the fill bath would cover every surface in the compressor room, including the roof over three metres above my head, and me from head to toe.

Luckily the rule was 'always wear ear muffs when filling dive cylinders', or I'd be deaf by now. The compressor room was always a noisy place to be, and O-rings blowing added to the noise significantly.

During the warm summer months from December to February, when people do the most diving, I'd fill dive cylinders for eight hours on end. The odd O-ring slippage would be welcomed with arms wide open, as the temperature would often top 30°C. After soaking up all the water off the floor with a dozen old towels and wiping the walls down, I'd be bone dry again, apart from sweat trickling down my spine, as well as beading the inside of my legs – yuck!

In my first year of working at the Dive Centre, I spent most of my time out the back of the shop filling dive cylinders and cleaning and fixing LPG (liquid petroleum gas) cylinders – the kind you use with your barbeque. I really wanted to be out the front selling dive equipment and talking to people about diving, because that was all that was on my mind.

Term three at school was action-packed, with two major focuses being rock climbing and kayaking. For the first half of the term we studied rock climbing and the last half we studied kayaking. I wasn't much of a rock climber, but soon learned the ropes (excuse the pun!).

There were many knots and safety procedures we had to learn before we abseiled off the side of one of the main buildings at school. Halfway down the main building, I stopped and waved at a class of third formers who were staring at us in utter disbelief from a nearby classroom. There was no trip away for rock climbing, but we spent quite a few hours in the local rocknasium sharpening up our handholds and rope skills.

When the teacher briefly left the class, one of our favourite activities was to challenge a friend to a game of 'around the table'. The game starts with someone lying stomach-down on a table. The objective is to get underneath the table, around to the opposite side and back on top of the table again – without touching the ground! I was never too good at it but some of my wiry mates managed to get around a table in under ten seconds.

There weren't too many places we could practise kayaking at school, as we didn't have a pool. I suggested testing our skills with some speed-sliding in the kayaks down the seriously steep grassy hill leading to the top field. The relief teacher didn't take my silly comment too well but I got full support from my classmates!

A few times a week our class headed down to Castor Bay, a small local beach, where an instructor taught us kayaking basics. At least half of each lesson was typically spent surfing small waves over a shallow rocky reef. Out of all the activities we had done so far for outdoor education, kayaking was the sport I was the least excited by. I think it was because we just sat in the kayaks, learnt a few skills and didn't go anywhere exciting. It would have been great if we went on a kayaking trip to some exotic coastline, but, as per normal, we didn't have the time for that.

In term four, we took up a sport that I was most excited by – shooting. Before any of us laid our hands on a gun, we had to learn the gun safety code and be tested. It was common sense, so most of the class passed, and we were on the way to the school's music block – yep, the music block.

Initially I thought we were about to do some stupid gun imitation sound with instruments, yet that couldn't have been further from the truth. Instead we were taken to a heavily locked door, which led to stairs that took us underneath the music block. There we were each handed a .22 rifle with live ammunition – how awesome is that?! I was so excited, I'm surprised Mr Mullins even handed me a gun.

You'd think that we would have gone to a rifle range, but no. Our school must be the only high school in the world with a shooting range underneath its music block!

At the firing end of the range were two large platforms, one above the other (similar to a huge bunk bed) where half a dozen people could shoot at once. The target end was lined with thick concrete and covered with phone books to slow the bullets. We all wore earmuffs, as the noise was deafening when we were all shooting at once. On more than one occasion I'm sure the poor music students were thrown out of tune by the erratic sound of gun shots from below them.

Luckily for the music students, the school has since had major renovations. Unfortunately for the outdoor education students, the renovations included a brand new auditorium and the rifle range had to be shut down because the auditorium was built over the top of it.

I finished my sixth form year with nineteen points. If I had scored twenty-one, I would have failed the year (as, in this instance, higher points meant lower achievement). My best mark for sixth form was, without surprise, outdoor education. At school I was never very academic, with most of my grades falling between forty and sixty per cent. Most of the time in class, I quickly lost interest in subjects unless they were somehow related to snorkelling, scuba diving or the bush. However, if I tried hard, like I did in outdoor education, I proved to myself that I could get good grades.

My last year at school was seventh form. It was the best of all my years at school, but probably the least academic. When looking back to my seventh form year, I'm so glad I stayed at school. The friendships I made, the opportunities that came my way, and the camaraderie between my large group of friends provided a priceless, one-off, once-in-a-lifetime experience that I'll never forget. The subjects I took were science, applied maths (I called it vege-maths because it was far easier than the standard maths), economics, computing and outdoor recreation. At the beginning of the year I was selected by the teachers and seventh form students to be one of the school prefects. I definitely wasn't chosen for my academic ability, rather I had a good attitude towards teachers, students, sports and school life in general. I was polite, friendly and not a troublemaker, but still had some fun with food fights and practical jokes, and always tried to bring the humour out in every situation – with no harm intended. Prefects have certain privileges over other students and are leaders and role models. We had our own line to the tuckshop, so we could buy food ten times quicker than anyone else, and our own car park – major privileges back then!

The last day ever of school approached too quickly. In the past, thoughts of leaving school seemed the best thing ever. But when it came down to the last week, I didn't really want to leave. It was sad. Once I started work, I'd be working an eight-hour day instead of doing a six-hour day at school. If I was continuously late to work I could get fired, whereas in school I would have been given a detention, which was nothing compared to losing a job. I wouldn't see my friends every day – that was the biggest negative aspect of leaving school.

Like everything, there were positives and negatives to leaving school, and I couldn't stay at school forever, although I'd have liked to! I'll always remember and be grateful for the fun and hilarious times I had at school, as well as the priceless lifelong friendships I developed, the successful sport teams I was part of, and the positive culture and environment of Westlake Boys High School that shaped me into the person I am today.

Towards the end of seventh form came the time when I needed to decide what I wanted to do once I left school. I had many conversations with Mum and Dad, discussing possible jobs and careers paths. The problem was that I didn't have any idea of what path I wanted to take. Mum and Dad said they would support me with whatever I chose to do. The only thing my dad stressed to me was the importance of getting a trade. He believed it was vital to learn a trade or become qualified in a profession. It didn't matter what that was: a plumber, a builder, a policeman or attending university to get a degree. Dad reminded me that once qualified, if I decided I didn't like the job or wanted to head overseas, I could always go back later to the job that I was qualified to do and could earn a reasonable wage or salary.

Still, I couldn't find anything that I felt committed to doing and was passionate about. Choosing a career path or profession is not a decision that should be taken lightly. Attending university is very costly and there's no way you want to be studying for or working in a job you don't enjoy. With input from Mum and Dad, I decided I would take a year to think about what I wanted to do with my life and, if possible, work at the Dive Centre.

One day before school finished, the manager from the Dive Centre asked what I wanted to do once I left school. Thinking, Gee, I really hope he asks me to work full-time, I said to him, 'Ah nothing, I don't have any plans yet.'

And I heard the words I'd been hoping for.

'Would you like to have a full-time position with us here at the Dive Centre?'

I was stoked that I had something I actually wanted to do once I left school so it didn't take me long to consider his offer.

'Thanks, I'd love to!'

Working at the Dive Centre appealed because I knew I'd learn some new skills and have some fun, while thinking about what I really wanted to do long term.

Taking my 'gap year', as some call it, turned out to be one of the best choices I have ever made. It gave me the time to seriously consider all the options up for grabs in the big wide world of work. And hey, I was only eighteen years old – I was just a baby, and there was no rush to make big career decisions. Plus it was the first time that I was earning money full time – I wanted to live it up, have fun and enjoy life.

CHAPTER FIVE

INTENDED TONGARIRO TRAVERSE – DAY TWO

*If you're not living life on the edge,
you're taking up too much space.*
UNKNOWN – TOLD TO ME BY
MY UNCLE, IAN PIKE

After a comfortable night's sleep, I woke on 25 September 2007, not knowing that this would be the last day that I would ever walk on my two legs.

James and I decided to pack our bags and walk up to the Ruapehu Hut to cook and eat with our friends. Cooking a meal indoors, without gloves, wind or snow, is a real treat. I didn't take cooking indoors for granted, as I knew the next few days would throw the hardships of cooking outdoors right at us.

The porridge went down a treat, then we repacked our packs and stepped outside. The first thing I felt was the warmth of the sun, so I immediately took off my jacket and stuffed it on the outside of my pack next to my crampons. A couple of the guys we knew from the Ruapehu Hut were outside the hut clowning around, lying on the snow in their undies and posing for photos. It was quite funny, but they must have been blimmin' cold.

Walking away from the hut and looking up the mountain to the approximate position of the Dome Shelter caused a

INTENDED TONGARIRO TRAVERSE – DAY TWO

small knot of nervousness to tighten inside me. I had never been to the Dome Shelter before and wanted to get there early in case we had trouble finding it. Having stayed in other huts at high altitude, I knew there was a high chance of the hut being completely iced over. I also thought about the amount of time we'd need to pitch a tent or dig a snow cave if we decided not to sleep in the shelter.

As the terrain steepened, I started to slow down. James was behind me, and I decided to keep going at a steady pace until I reached a certain point, where I would wait for James to catch up. I find it easier to walk at my own steady pace for hours than to slow it down.

As I stopped for James I thought, I can't remember a time when the sun was so ferocious. It was intensified by the fact that the wind wasn't blowing. I opened all the vents in my pants and unzipped the thermal layer next to my skin. My beanie had been in my pocket since we left the hut. Sweat continued to run down my forehead until it met the foam on my snow goggles. Eventually the sweat build up got too much for the foam and it dripped through onto my eyelashes. The sweat that collected on my eyelashes began to paint the inside of my snow goggles, like a car's perished window wipers smearing water across the windscreen.

I stopped to wait for James and peered through my blurry ski goggles across to the Pinnacles, which stood staunchly in the morning light. I felt so privileged to be in an environment that offers lifelong memories, once-in-a-lifetime sights and incredible opportunities.

We continued climbing together amongst intermittent cloud that would completely obscure our view for a minute or two then totally clear again. James and I made sure we knew exactly where we were on the map and would frequently double check our position with a global positioning system (GPS).

As we gained altitude the wind started to pick up – it was a welcome relief from the scorching heat. The crisp wind cut through my thermals like a razor-sharp knife and chilled the surface of my skin. Thinking the wind would drop again, I waited to put my windproof jacket on. Minutes passed and I began to shiver, and my jacket went back on smartly. The speed at which the temperature can drop in the mountains still amazes me.

The terrain steepened as we approached the notch, which gives easy access to the summit plateau. I was a bit worried about the hard snow underfoot, and James and I agreed to put our crampons on if the snow got any harder. I've learnt that communication is super-important in high-risk situations. The other person may see something in a different way or have a different approach to a problem. I always like to discuss the options and make joint decisions where possible.

I could see the geological shape of the Dome but no Dome Shelter yet. My map confirmed we were heading in the right direction, so we followed a spur that lead up to the right and around to the left, before joining onto the prominent Dome.

Fifteen or more minutes passed and still no sign of the Dome Shelter. I told James I was a bit concerned. After many trips navigating with a compass and map I've learnt to trust my map, even when I think it might be wrong. The map is never wrong, it's my map-reading skills that can be wrong. James was a bit unsure so to ease the tension I bet him ten bucks that the shelter would be just over the Dome.

By now, we were both a bit tired and cold. The temperature had dropped rapidly and made the sweat on my skin feel icy cold. All the vents on my pants and jacket were now done up. My hood covered my head and with the protection of my helmet, beanie and snow goggles, only my nose and lips were exposed to the stiff and bitter breeze.

Sure enough, soon I could see a large chunk of wind-blown ice that could possibly be the Dome Shelter. I dropped my pack and told James to wait while I checked to see if we were at the hut. With my pack off, I instantly felt weightless, so bounded across the firm snow like an astronaut on the moon.

I was holding my ice axe in my left hand as I tried to make out anything man-made lying in or under the ice. Out of nowhere a small triangular wooden building greeted me. The shelter was nearly swallowed whole by snow and ice. The door, three-quarters buried in snow, needed to be dug out with a shovel before we could get in. Hopefully it was just snow, not thick ice, or we may not get into the hut! The shelter was a truly impressive display of Mother Nature's ability to transform a simple building into a breathtaking snow and ice masterpiece. I was speechless as I inspected the hut more closely and felt my excitement reach a new level.

With a gaping grin on my face and adrenaline flowing through my system, I zoomed back to where James was waiting with my pack and said, 'You owe me ten bucks mate!'

I don't think James cared about his new debt as he let out a yelp and most likely felt a great sense of relief. Before I heaved my pack onto my back again I slung my camera around my neck, ready to capture this unbelievable landscape.

Standing in front of the shelter for a second time, I was struck by its extraordinary location and its overwhelming views. Then, and even now, no words of mine could describe the awe-inspiring landscape that surrounded us. Not surprisingly, James was speechless too.

After a few moments taking it all in, I said to James, 'Let's dig it out and see what she's like inside eh?'

He replied, 'Yeah, yeah – let's get to work.'

We removed our shovels from our packs and began to

shift the large quantity of snow blocking the door – and luckily there was no ice. I tried to be crafty and shape a stairway in the snow leading into the hut. The snow was dry like powder, and it didn't work too well – it just crumpled under our boots.

I removed the large steel bar that kept the door firmly shut and placed it in soft snow to the left of the door. With two hands I gave the door a big shove. Nothing happened. I did the same again, with the help of my shoulder, and managed to make the door budge a little. Another two-handed push and the icy seal between the door and the shelter busted free and the door swung open inwards to the right.

Nice, but basic, was my first impression. 'If we don't end up pitching a tent or digging a snow cave, this looks cosy enough.'

Luckily James and I were easily pleased and fully equipped to survive anywhere in the mountain environment. A quick inspection of the shelter confirmed what I had been thinking. It had no lights, no heating, no beds or bedding, no toilet, no kitchen sink, no cooking facilities, no power, no communication devices, no windows and just that one seat, plus a shovel. The floor and walls were made of well-worn plywood. The floor was full of tiny holes from people's crampon spikes and the walls were dotted with hooks and nails to hang items from. An escape hatch similar to a short fat chimney in the upper right-hand corner of the first room provided an alternative entry in case the door was completely covered with rock-hard snow or bulletproof ice. On this occasion it was the escape hatch that was hidden under a metre of solid ice. The main door was our only means of entering and exiting the hut.

Standing still inside the hut, out of direct sunlight, we began to get cold very quickly. As always, it was my hands and feet that began to feel the dull sting of the cold. James and I sipped on our water bottles and scoffed a muesli bar each and some chocolate. I had to chew the frozen chocolate and muesli bar ten times more than is normally required at sea-level temperatures.

As part of the main objective of our trip, we wanted to climb all three prominent peaks in the Tongariro National Park. The closest and first peak we were going to attempt was Tahurangi, the true summit of Mt Ruapehu, sitting just shy of 3000 metres at 2797 metres. The shelter was the ideal place to climb Tahurangi from.

I opted to empty my pack and take some emergency gear for both of us. There was no point in James carrying a pack too. I took my down jacket, sleeping bag, first aid kit, sleeping pad, drink bottle, two muesli bars and a shovel. If we got lost we could dig a snow cave, lie on the sleeping pad and both keep warm in my sleeping bag. The same gear could be used if one of us got injured.

I packed the emergency gear in my pack without any gloves on – bad move. My hands were seriously cold now. However, I was confident they would warm up as soon as we got moving. I opened the door and scrambled up the crumpling stairway to heaven. The stairway didn't lead us to heaven, but it sure did seem like it – the picture-perfect landscape dominated as far as the eye could see.

As soon as I was out of the shade, the sun's warmth filled me with energy and forced blood back into my hands and feet – it felt great.

James and I had planned to walk in a southwesterly direction via an unnamed peak at 2757 metres to reach the summit of Tahurangi. Before reaching the unnamed peak, James and I were passing bitter comments under our breath about the unbelievably soft snow conditions. Our feet were sinking through the snow up to our knees. The snow slowed our progress, which was a bit of a worry as I wanted to be back at the Dome Shelter well before dark. The soft snow conditions here made me wonder about what the snow conditions would be like along the razor-sharp ridge that led to Tahurangi.

As we started up towards the unnamed peak, my concerns increased. To our left there was a sheer drop of sixty metres – or thereabouts – to the calm-looking crater lake. To our right was a forty-five-degree slope with a very long but relatively good run out if one or both of us were to slip and fall.

I told James that I was unhappy with the current snow conditions, but we should keep going for another hundred metres and then reassess. James agreed.

One hundred metres later I made the decision to terminate the climb. I made the call because the snow was crumpling away with even the slightest pressure from our boots and ice axes. At one stage I swung my ice axe pick first into the ice, which shattered into a thousand bits, like a glass cup being dropped from a two-storey building.

It was a hard decision to make; we were so close to the summit and wouldn't achieve our trip objective if we stopped now. Feeling frustrated, I recalled an old mountain saying: the mountain is not going anywhere, it will still be there another day. That great saying relates to other ventures of life and can be applied in the exact same way. It's never worth risking your life to climb a peak if the conditions aren't right, because there will always be another opportunity to climb the mountain.

James agreed with my decision to terminate the climb and was quite eager to try out my suggested plan B. Plan B involved descending a little, unrolling my sleeping mat and relaxing on it. Perfect.

Five minutes later we were lying spread out like reptiles soaking up as much of the sun's remaining warmth as possible. To the west I could quite clearly see Mt Taranaki, on the west coast. It was quite ironic, we were sunbathing in mountaineering equipment and clothing at approximately 2600 metres. What an amazing feeling! There was a high chance we were higher up than anyone else in the North Island – except people in aeroplanes of course.

Staring into the distance, I began to feel free of everyday expectations. No need to answer a phone call, email or text message. I could eat, sleep and wake whenever I pleased. I was happy in my little world, which I shared only with James. I felt like an ancient explorer discovering a new civilisation. Imagine that!

The cold wind and air temperature at 2600 metres finally got the better of us, forcing us to get moving again to warm up. I repacked my pack and started the slow plod in soft snow back to the Dome Shelter.

At the top of small slope, James and I discussed our sleeping arrangements. Neither of us liked the idea of tenting at this altitude without an up-to-date weather forecast, so we crossed that option off the list. Wind at this altitude is unpredictable and could destroy our tent without warning. Our night would be miserable if we had to spend half of it digging a snow cave to replace our munted tent.

Snow caving was very possible; it would be a safer and warmer option than tenting, but it would require two or three hours of hard work. With an early start tomorrow morning planned, James and I agreed that we'd get an early night's sleep in the Dome Shelter and get away quickly in the morning.

The last one hundred metres to the Dome Shelter was an uphill battle in awfully soft snow. On entering the shelter I flicked my headlamp on and was glad I had worked up a sweat, as I felt like I had just entered a dark freezer.

Excited at the thought and challenge of cooking dinner outside, I offered to cook tonight. James was pleased and said he would tidy our equipment scattered throughout the hut – fair deal I thought.

I replaced my beanie with a balaclava and swapped my thin gloves for my toasty warm, thicker polar fleece gloves. I put on my down jacket for extra warmth. These extra clothes were all necessary – I planned to be outside in the cold for at least an hour, which is how long it would take me to melt water for tomorrow and cook tonight's dinner.

I opened the main door and clambered outside. On the way out of the shelter my left glove got stuck on a piece of metal attached to the hut. I had to blow on it with warm air from my mouth to free it. The little bit of moisture, probably spilt from my drink bottle, had managed to freeze my glove to the metal.

Gee, it'd be a good idea to keep my tongue away from that! Hopefully my spoon doesn't do the same when I'm eating dinner, I thought to myself.

Once I got free and got right outside, I could see the crater lake. I stopped for a second just to take it all in. It was tranquil, peaceful and unthreatening.

One concern that plays on your mind when in the mountains is hypothermia. You'll understand shortly why I'm explaining this now. Hypothermia is a very serious and common condition caused by your body getting too cold and your body temperature dropping below the normal 37°C. If you don't have sufficient clothing protection in extremely cold temperatures, hypothermia will eventually set in.

The symptoms experienced at the temperatures listed below are a guide only. Different people may experience symptoms before or after someone else at the same body temperature. If body temperature drops one degree, the victim will begin shivering and numbness in the arms and legs will begin to develop. At 35°C the victim is considered to have mild hypothermia and will be shivering uncontrollably. Their hands and feet will appear numb.

The victim may seem clumsy, irrational and confused as the body reaches 34°C. Performing simple tasks with hands and feet becomes difficult. Eventually the hands and feet become numb as blood withdraws into the chest and brain, where it is needed most. The victim can look pale, with their fingers, toes and lips all turning blue. Breathing becomes shallow and quick. They will also be shivering uncontrollably.

At 33°C a victim is considered to have moderate hypothermia. As well as the other symptoms above, their muscles will be getting stiff.

At 32°C a phenomenon known as a warming sensation can be experienced by the victim. They may feel as though they are getting warmer, and possibly escaping the effects of hypothermia. This is a false feeling associated with severe hypothermia.

When the hypothermia is this severe, and with the body temperature around 31°C, the victim may collapse and become semi-conscious.

At 30°C the victim is considered to have critical hypothermia. A victim with critical hypothermia will be unconscious and not respond to pain. Their skin will be very cold to touch and may appear a bluish grey colour.

With a body temperature of 29°C, the victim will have a very slow pulse and it might be difficult to detect breathing.

At 28°C and below, a cardiac arrest is likely to occur. This is also known as a heart attack and is when the heart stops beating. There may be no obvious pulse or breathing. The victim's pupils might be dilated and fixed, and they may appear dead.

The many complications of moving and rewarming a very hypothermic victim need to be fully understood before attempting to do so. Rewarming a victim must be done extremely slowly. Putting a patient in a hot bath or shower will draw their blood to the skin's surface, taking it away from vital organs – death can occur from sudden rewarming. Also, the smallest bump or knock to the patient can stop their heart, so extreme care is required when handling a very cold patient.

CHAPTER SIX

EXPLORING INNER SPACE

From birth, man carries the weight of gravity on his shoulders. He is bolted to earth. But man has only to sink beneath the surface and he is free.
JACQUES YVES COUSTEAU

My passions of scuba diving and mountaineering complement each other perfectly. Summer is a good time to go scuba diving, but no good for mountaineering as there's no snow. In winter it's a bit chilly for scuba diving but ideal for mountaineering.

Besides water polo, scuba diving was my number one interest in my last year of high school and, unsurprisingly, for the few years that I worked at the Dive Centre. Before work, at work and after work I'd be getting on to the internet and checking when the weather would be good for a dive.

It was difficult to go diving on weekdays because I worked long hours, except on Wednesday, my day off. Just about every Wednesday I'd be out diving on a charter boat or on our family boat. Our boat is called *Floyd* after Pink Floyd, and its name is written on it in pink. *Floyd* is a fourteen-foot tinny (aluminium boat) with a forty-horsepower engine. It moves along at a good speed, just over forty kilometres per hour, even when fully laden with diving equipment. Whenever I go diving I take a boatman to act as a safety person, which in most cases is my brother, Andrew. If a diver gets into trouble,

Andrew can phone or radio via a VHF (very high frequency) radio for emergency services, or if a strong current carries one of us away from the dive site, it's Andrew's job to pick the diver up.

On Sunday the Dive Centre didn't open until 10 a.m. If we planned it in advance, my brother, one of my mates and I would get up at 4 a.m., leave the house at 4.30 a.m., and have our boat in the water up at Gulf Harbour marina by 5.30 a.m. We'd be under the water before 6.30 and we'd surface by 7.30. As long as we had the boat on the trailer by 8.30, I'd make it to work before 10 a.m. It was the best start to the day I could think of!

Gulf Harbour, at the end of Whangaparaoa Peninsula, is an easy forty-minute drive north from my house. From there it's a thirty-minute boat ride out to Tiritiri Matangi Island (also known as Tiri), which offers good diving and the chance of grabbing a crayfish or two if you look carefully. On Sundays before work, Tiri was often the dive site of choice.

One Sunday morning before work, I went diving with my friend, Brad Stephens and my brother Andrew. It was a beautifully clear morning with no wind and there was a good weather forecast for the entire day. We left Gulf Harbour just after 5.30 a.m. The water was oily calm and so inviting as the sun peered brightly over the horizon. As we motored at full speed out to Tiri we forced our way into our tight, thick wetsuits, which began to feel more like boiler suits as the sun's rays warmed us. We were really excited so there was no mucking around. As soon as Andrew dropped the anchor over the top of our dive site, Brad and I put on the rest of our diving equipment and jumped overboard.

The visibility was about ten to fifteen metres, which is great for the location. Plenty of fish were darting around, providing some good photo opportunities. I'd left my camera at home so I could focus on crayfish hunting.

I unclipped my cray snare from the carabiner on my BCD (buoyancy compensating device) attachment point and held it in my right hand. A cray snare is a retractable wire loop, about the size of a small dinner plate, on the end of a thin metal tube about a metre long. At the end is a handle. If you do it carefully, you can push the handle to open the loop up as big as it can go. Then if you move it directly towards the crayfish, firstly over its feelers, and then around its body, and pull the handle really fast – you should have it in the snare. Effectively, you will have lassoed the crayfish. If you manage to pull it out of its hole before it jams itself between some rocks, you'll have a crayfish on your dinner plate at the end of the day!

As I stuck my head into a dark hole, I heard the sound of a motor buzzing about on the surface. I thought, No, it can't be *Floyd*. Or, maybe Andrew's being stupid and racing the boat around. Geez, I'll give him an earful when we surface. I hope he stops it before we reach the surface or else he's likely to chop one of us to bits with the propeller. Oh well, I'll listen out for the noise when we surface.

I illuminated a dark hole with my powerful dive torch: no crays, just a few fish, probably having a nap in the dark. I swam horizontally, with a large wall of kelp and rocks to my left and Brad trailing behind me. He was searching frantically in every hole, crack and crevice, just like a dog madly searching for a bone. Brad loves eating crayfish and loves getting them.

We had been underwater for about twenty minutes, and I could still hear some boat buzzing round on the surface. I shone my torch through a thick kelp forest and into a vertical crevice. The feelers of a crayfish caught my eye. I was on to something here! I could feel my heart begin to beat quickly and I sucked three or four deep breaths from my regulator. I felt like a cheetah about to go for the kill.

I backed off slightly and brought myself into a vertical standing position, a hover, with the sea floor appearing five or more metres below me. I did the peace sign to Brad then touched the back of my hand against my forehead – that's our signal to mean there's crayfish. I saw bubbles explode from Brad's regulator; he was excited too!

Ever so carefully, I extended the snare in front of me directly towards the crayfish. The crayfish's feelers began to twitch, sensing the water's movement created by my slowly approaching snare. Over the feelers ... around the body ... and ... pull! I got it!

As I withdrew the crayfish from its crevice, it came into better view, and it was big, about the size of a cat. The crayfish began to snap its tail, tugging powerfully on the snare and forcing me to tighten my grip so as not to let go. I felt Brad unclip my catch bag from my other BCD attachment point. The crayfish was trying to take off like a hungry great dane chasing a rabbit.

Luckily Brad had the catch bag wide open and I wrestled the crayfish into the bottom of the bag, loosened the cray snare and shut the catch bag. I gave Brad an underwater high five – great teamwork!

Yes! We had bagged one! I looked down at my air gauge. I noticed that I had sucked through quite a bit of air with all the excitement.

Brad swam in front of me and I followed him. The underwater landscape quickly changed. As far as I could see there were huge kelp-covered boulders the size of cars sitting in the sand. Brad began checking in likely places for crayfish. In the background I could still hear a boat roaring above us – it seemed louder.

It wasn't long before Brad spotted a crayfish. I could easily tell, as he shook with excitement and, again, bubbles exploded from his regulator. Brad, as a tradesman, prefers to use his hands to catch crayfish instead of a snare. I laughed to myself as Brad went to snatch the crayfish from its home with his hand. His fins were all over the place, thrashing about – anyone would have thought some kind of killer eel was dragging him into its hole, not that Brad was trying to pull a crayfish out of a hole! All that thrashing around stirred up silt and sand, totally obscuring Brad from my view. Seconds later he appeared, flustered and without a crayfish.

As we were nearing the safety reserve of air in our tanks, Brad managed to pluck a crayfish from its home and we put it with its friend in my catch bag. I was concerned about the boat still buzzing around the surface because we had to begin to ascend. But we didn't have a choice; we had hardly any air left.

Without reason, Brad began to swim directly for the bottom. I wondered what he was doing – he had hardly any air left. As soon as he'd touched the bottom he slowly began to surface towards me. He waved a torch at me; it wasn't his. Then I clicked – he must have seen the torch and descended to get it. What a score, it was a nice torch too!

My hands broke the surface first, then my head. I turned in a circle to spot the noisy boat. It was Andrew in *Floyd*, about 200 metres to my right. 'What on earth is going on?' I asked Brad. He didn't reply. He was busy marvelling at his new torch.

Andrew must have seen us surface, because he turned *Floyd* in our direction and slowed as he approached us. Before I could say anything Andrew started yelling.

'Oi! You dork, you forgot to put the bung in and water began to cover the floorboards just as you went underwater. I didn't know what to do, apart from drive the boat as fast as I could to let the water drain back out the bung hole!'

I was shocked – but happy *Floyd* wasn't on the bottom of the ocean with the other crayfish.

'Good thinking,' I said. 'Drive closer, stop the engine and I'll screw the bung in.'

Luckily the bung was still attached to the boat with a piece of string. I screwed it back in, feeling very relieved.

We clambered back on the boat and measured the crayfish to ensure they were the legal size. They were all over the limit, especially the one Brad got.

Brad and I discussed the things we'd seen on the dive, while Andrew hauled the anchor up. Andrew slowly accelerated us to full speed. On the way back to the boat ramp, the only sound was a lovely 'hiss hiss' from the water as it was displaced by *Floyd*'s bow every time the boat went over a small swell. We had smiles on our faces, warm wind blowing through our salty hair and crayfish for tea, and we felt extremely lucky that we weren't swimming home! I was looking forward to work and sharing the highlights of our dive with customers.

Working full-time at the Dive Centre, I naturally learnt a lot about scuba diving. I learnt how every single item of scuba diving equipment works, how to fix it, how much it costs and how to tell quality products from cheap products. I never hesitated in spending money on equipment that would keep me alive when underwater. Having so much knowledge about scuba diving was fantastic when I was out in or on the water. I felt safe and confident – that's the beauty of working with the things you love. Another beauty is cheap equipment. When you're working in a retail outlet you usually get an amazing discount on the products you sell. If you have a passion, like mountain biking or surfing, try to get a job in a bike shop or surf shop – you'll learn heaps and get cheap bikes or boards!

As with everything, there was a downside. The downside of working with the things I loved is that after a while when

I wanted some time out to get away from work for a day, I'd end up going diving. I generally enjoyed my work but sometimes I felt that it was important to give my mind a rest from the same old thing each day. Sometimes I wished I could keep my work separate from my hobbies. Finding the right balance between the two was the key.

Another downside to working in a retail outlet is the hours you work. Most retail outlets are open from 8.30 a.m. or 9 a.m. and don't close until 5 p.m. or 6 p.m. And they're usually open in the weekend, which is often the busiest time of the week. What you'll find is that when you're working full-time in a retail store, you'll have to work weekends and you'll have one or two days off in the middle of the week. So in the weekend all my mates would go to the beach or go away somewhere and I was stuck at work. The same happened mid-week; I'd want to go to the beach or head away but my friends would all be at work or at university and I didn't want to go by myself. You can't have everything though, a compromise here and there is important.

While there were some things I didn't like about working in retail, there were some great things about it too. One key thing is that I learnt retail skills. I'll never regret that. Retail skills are very broad. Approaching a customer and talking to them about your products isn't as easy as you think. Trying to be a salesperson to complete a sale and being friendly at the same time takes some practice. I learnt communication skills at the Dive Centre that have served me well since. Making telephone calls, and writing emails, notes or letters needs to be done differently from how you'd do them at home. Answering the phone, I'd say 'Thanks for calling Dive Centre, William speaking, how can I help you?' That's so much better than just saying, 'Hi, Dive Centre.'

I've also learnt and developed people skills, which I class

as ultra-important and really useful. People skills can be the way you approach a customer, like, 'Hello sir, how are you today? Is there anything I can help you with or are you happy looking around?' That's better than saying, 'Hi. Can I help you?' – that's boring and shows you're not taking much of an interest in the customer.

Dealing with unhappy customers can be difficult but it's a great skill to learn. If you can calm them down, assess their problem quickly (and help cheer them up if possible), hopefully the customer will return to the shop again, spend more money, and not go away telling others how terrible they thought the service was – even if they'd had great service.

I found that, at the end of the day, a good salesperson will make money for the store. Retail skills and knowledge of the product you are selling is critical. If you work in a retail store, develop good people and retail skills, read up on the products you sell and you'll be away laughing!

Working at a scuba diving shop, you'd think I'd get to do a fair bit of diving – you're right. I loved it! The easiest way to explain what scuba diving is like is to think of space. It seems like you are defying the rules of gravity and nature, and you can survive in an environment where humans aren't meant to. You are totally weightless and can fly wherever you wish. You hear nothing but the bubbles trickling past your ears and tickling your face as they are expelled from your regulator. Amongst the giant caves, spectacular-looking gardens and canyon walls, you feel like a tiny spaceship surrounded with billions of sparkling colours darting about. Then all of a sudden your surroundings can completely change as you swim off a drop-off that plummets a hundred metres into an inky-black abyss. All you can see is a deep blue void surrounding you. Once you lose sight of the rocks or kelp swaying in the current, the only two ways you can tell which way is up are to look at your bubbles and follow your depth gauge.

Every dive is different, even if you have dived at the specific location before. Good or bad visibility can totally transform the dive from a muddy quarry to a tropical delight. The muddy brown-looking kelp that you passed a few weeks ago might have morphed into a dazzling multicoloured collection of tiny growths, sponges and microscopic animals living and feeding under the protective kelp forest.

You could easily spend an hour inspecting two or three square metres of seabed or seawall, identifying hundreds of different plants and animals. You're never short of a few surprises either – moray eels poking their heads out from their homes and inspecting you, the strange object passing their front door. Or you might come eye to eye with a two- or three-metre-long stingray as you glide over a rocky outcrop – that sure makes you suck on your regulator!

The underwater world is a photographer's dream, with photo opportunities left, right and centre. Some of the best photos I have ever seen have been taken underwater. The diversity of colours and marine life is simply stunning. Looking at the underwater photos in magazines and on the walls at the Dive Centre inspired me to save up for an underwater camera. Scuba diving is already expensive, as it is an equipment-intensive sport, without adding thousands of dollars of photographic equipment. My underwater camera kit consisted of a waterproof hard case for transporting the camera to and from dive sites, a three-megapixel camera with a waterproof polycarbonate casing, a strobe, a polycarbonate base to attach the camera and strobe, and a twenty-millimetre lens for wide-angle shots. The kit sold for slightly under the enormous amount of $5000 in 2003. However, there is simply no cheap way with underwater photography. If you want to get good shots you've got to have good equipment that can handle the extreme pressure of the sea water at depth.

Once I got my underwater camera, I was hooked on underwater photography. All I wanted to do was get on a fast boat, zoom out to a pristine dive site and dive all day long. I experimented with different angles, different light and different lenses.

Once I was familiar with my camera, I took some pretty sharp shots for a young amateur. My favourite dive site for photography is, without a doubt, the Poor Knights Islands, twenty-one kilometres by sea from Tutukaka Harbour in Northland. The islands are rated as one of the top ten dive sites in the world!

From Auckland it's a two-and-a-half-hour drive north. The islands are made up of two large islands with a dozen or so small islands sitting close to them. The islands are about eleven million years old and are the remains of extinct volcanoes, well worn by the continual beating of the powerful ocean waves.

Beyond the Poor Knights lies the Pacific Ocean; next stop from the islands would be somewhere in South America! It can get pretty rough out there, and there is usually a sizeable swell, so you need a large boat to dive from. The Department of Conservation (DOC) prohibits anyone from landing on any of the islands, as they are home to many tuatara. Tuatara are lizard-like creatures that have been around since the time of the dinosaurs. They are only found in New Zealand.

From the high-tide mark to the seabed and 800 metres out to sea from each of the islands is a marine reserve. No fishing, feeding or taking anything from the ocean inside a marine reserve is allowed. Heavy penalties, including fines and jail, are enforced if anyone takes any type of marine life from the reserve. Outside of marine reserves, you are free to take marine life according to the Ministry of Fisheries rules and regulations while fishing or diving. I prefer taking photos, not marine life, but I've had some fun dives hunting for crayfish.

Scuba diving is sometimes perceived as a dangerous sport by those who aren't experienced divers. Like any sport, if the recommended guidelines are followed, the chances of a fatal accident are significantly decreased. By writing a list of all my dive equipment and checking safety procedures with my dive buddies, I've been lucky enough to not come across any major problems. When I write a list of all my dive gear, I check off each item as I pack it into my dive bag, making sure I don't forget anything important. Checking safety procedures off with my dive buddy means we both make sure we haven't forgotten anything. A simple equipment checklist and safety checks with a buddy or partner helps prevent accidents in all sports, not just diving. However, sometimes things can go wrong even when you do think and plan carefully.

The near-catastrophe caused by forgetting to do up *Floyd*'s bung could have been prevented with a simple checklist.

There was another near-catastrophe during a night dive I did at Leigh reef. I had heard other divers raving about what an awesome dive Leigh reef was. When I saw a scheduled night dive at Leigh reef on a charter boat, I didn't hesitate to put my name on the list. I also signed up my friend, Jesse McBride.

As the clock ticked 5.30 p.m. at work, Jesse was already waiting for me in the car park. We excitedly loaded up my van with our dive bags and cylinders, and headed north.

An hour later, we were slowly winding down the steep, narrow road leading us to the Leigh wharf. As we searched for a park I could see the dive boat. The skipper was skilfully manoeuvring the fifty-foot motor catamaran *Divercity*, making it look so easy as he slowly approached the wharf, spun around 180 degrees and gently touched the wharf on the starboard side.

Soon I had my dive bag slung over one shoulder and my ten-kilo weight belt slung over the other, and a dive tank in one hand. With such heavy weight I felt as though I could sink into the tar seal if I didn't keep walking to the end of the wharf.

Jesse and I placed our gear on the wharf next to *Divercity* and waited for others to arrive to form a chain gang. Once more people had arrived, we formed a human conveyer-belt by standing in a line from the pile of dive equipment on the wharf, down the stairs, and onto the boat's deck. We quickly got the boat loaded and were ready for departure. It was a lovely evening with light wind and a clear sky.

Leigh reef is only a ten-minute boat ride from the Leigh harbour. It took about five minutes of searching with a depth sounder to find the underwater reef. The Leigh reef is very deep, at around thirty metres, making it near impossible to find without local knowledge or a depth sounder. Being deep and out of the harbour, the reef is prone to strong currents, so it's necessary to use a boat in case a diver is overcome by the currents. By the time the skipper began searching for the reef, Jesse and I had started the lengthy process of gearing up.

When getting geared up, the first thing I did was squeeze into my merino wool-lined wetsuit, slip on my wetsuit booties and do up my weight belt around my hips. Then I attached my dive cylinder to my BCD jacket and attached my regulators and dive computer to the dive cylinder. Next, I sat down and awkwardly struggled to put on my BCD, a process that is similar to trying to haul an overloaded tramping pack onto your back at the start of a seven-day hike through the hills. Feeling cumbersome and sweating profusely, I battled to put my feet into my fins and clip them up. By now, all I wanted to do was flop into the cool water, but I had a few more things to do. I spat three times into my mask and rubbed the spit all over the glass to help prevent it fogging underwater. I stuffed my gloves into my BCD pocket so that when I jumped overboard I could make any adjustments easily without the false sensation created by wearing thick wetsuit gloves. I clipped my knife into its sheath on my BCD and clipped my torch onto a D-ring on my BCD with a carabiner. I was ready and so was Jesse.

We did a quick check of each other's equipment.

'Air on, weight belt, regs working, torch, buckles – all go?'

'Yep, you?' Jesse replied.

I took a few quick breaths on my regulator and said, 'Air on, weight belt locked, regs good, torch and all buckles fastened.'

Gearing up is usually hard work, but with all my gear hanging off me like a Christmas tree, I felt a bit like a navy diver about to undertake one of my most difficult missions ever.

I told the skipper we were ready to dive. He recorded the time we entered the water as a safety precaution. He would also record the time when we returned. We waddled like ducks to the side of the boat, and Jesse leapt overboard first. I held my regulator in my left hand, with two fingers on each lens of my mask to stop it coming off when I entered the water. I took a breath from my regulator and leapt overboard with a giant stride, plummeting heavily into the deep blue water, causing millions of tiny bubbles to form and frantically make their way to the surface. The difficult task of gearing up instantly paid off – I was free, free from gravity and free to descend into the inner space.

I surfaced after a few seconds and I turned my head to see Jesse bobbing patiently in the water next to two other divers. I gave the OK sign to Jesse, followed by the thumbs down sign to indicate that I was ready to descend. Jesse did the same back to me and we both pulled the dump valve on our BCDs to release the buoyancy-providing air and immediately begin our descent. From then on the only way to communicate with each other underwater was through hand signals – you can't talk underwater!

I watched my dive computer with interest as we continued to descend at a rate of a metre every two seconds. Within 40 seconds I was ten metres above some jagged-looking rocks that must have been the top of Leigh reef. Already I was amazed at the prolific fish life. A school of around twenty large kingfish staunchly passed over my right shoulder. Our surroundings were beginning to dim quickly as the sun tried its best to filter its weak rays into the depth of the ocean. I reached for my torch, unclipped it and turned it on. Every rock, diver, bit of seaweed or fish in my torch beam was powerfully illuminated.

I levelled off at twenty-six metres and moved my body into a horizontal position. Then I did the OK sign to Jesse and he did it back to me – we were both happy.

I didn't have my camera with me this time – it is too difficult to focus it in the dark. Instead I was armed with my cray snare and catch bag. I ferreted about through some kelp looking for crayfish and was surprised at how active the fish had become in the near-dark conditions. I pointed the powerful beam of my torch into a terribly dark diagonal crack and lit up the feelers of a nice-sized crayfish. In less than thirty seconds it was in my catch bag – I was stoked!

I continued finning slowly, feeling very relaxed and thinking how grateful I was to be diving at night in great conditions, seeing the sealife becoming more active in the dim light.

Jesse was finning about two metres to my right when I noticed a stray torch beam from behind me. I knew it wasn't Jesse's. I stopped, turned around and lit up a lonesome diver. Seconds later this diver was within my reach. All I could tell

LEFT: Me at twelve years old on the trail back to the Shyangboche landing strip after having a cup of tea at the Hotel Everest View.
PHOTO: LAURIE PIKE

BELOW: The Westlake Boys High School premier water polo team: winners of the National Schoolboys Water Polo Championship for the third year in a row. We were dubbed the 'dream team'. Photo taken in April 2002, my seventh form year at Westlake.

ABOVE: Me standing on top of Castle Rock, at Castle Point in Wairarapa, December 2005. PHOTO: OLIVER PIKE

BELOW: Standing on the summit of Mt Tongariro (1967 metres), the first mountain I climbed, in October 2005. PHOTO: CAMERON WALKER

ABOVE: Me (on the left) with Cameron Walker. Taken at the saddle in between Mt Tongariro and Mt Ngauruhoe on the Tongariro crossing, before our first ascent of Mt Ngauruhoe. May 2006. PHOTO: TRIPOD

BELOW: The Dome Shelter on Mt Ruapehu on 25 September 2007 at approximately 3 p.m. James in the background. The hut is entirely encased in ice. PHOTO: WILLIAM PIKE

ABOVE: Me sitting on the shaft of a spade just after finishing a yummy dinner in the Dome Shelter at approximately 7 p.m. on 25 September 2007. Last photo of me with two fully functioning legs! PHOTO: JAMES CHRISTIE

RIGHT: Members of the Ruapehu Alpine Rescue Organisation (RARO) at the entrance of the Dome Shelter at approximately 1 a.m. on 26 September 2007, preparing to remove me from the shelter approximately five hours after the eruption of Mt Ruapehu.
PHOTO: NICKY HUGHES (SHORTY)

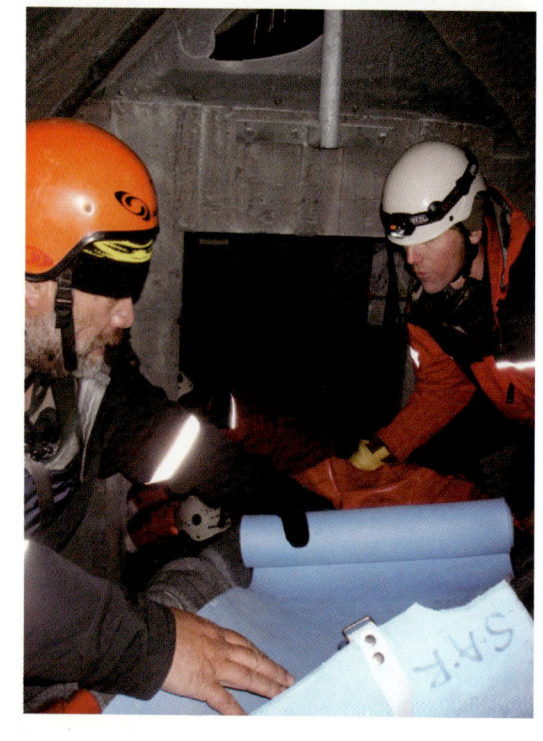

LEFT: Second compartment of the Dome Shelter. Note the height of the waterline in the upper left of the photo, and the mud/ash caught by the lip of wood, halfway down the waterline on the left and right walls. November 2007. PHOTO: ANDREW PIKE

BELOW: The first compartment (where we were sleeping) of the hut showing the Dome Shelter's entrance to the upper right. The floor completely collapsed under the weight of the mud, rocks, and water. While facing the entrance it is highly likely my right leg was snapped underneath the floorboard in the opposite direction to the entrance. Bits of my sleeping bag and James's pack liner (red/orange/black) were impossible to remove. November 2007. PHOTO: BARRY PIKE

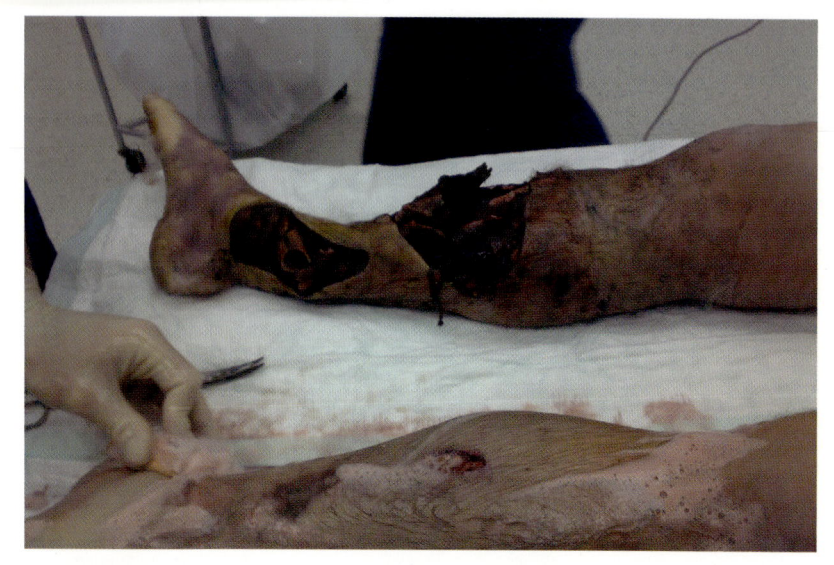

ABOVE: My damaged leg. Surgeons washing my left leg and preparing to amputate my right leg from below the knee. Note the colour of the right foot, indicating loss of circulation and death of tissue/foot.

BELOW: My hero James holding my hand, with his parents at my side. A critically ill William, early evening of 26 September 2007, after the amputation. PHOTO: TRACY PIKE

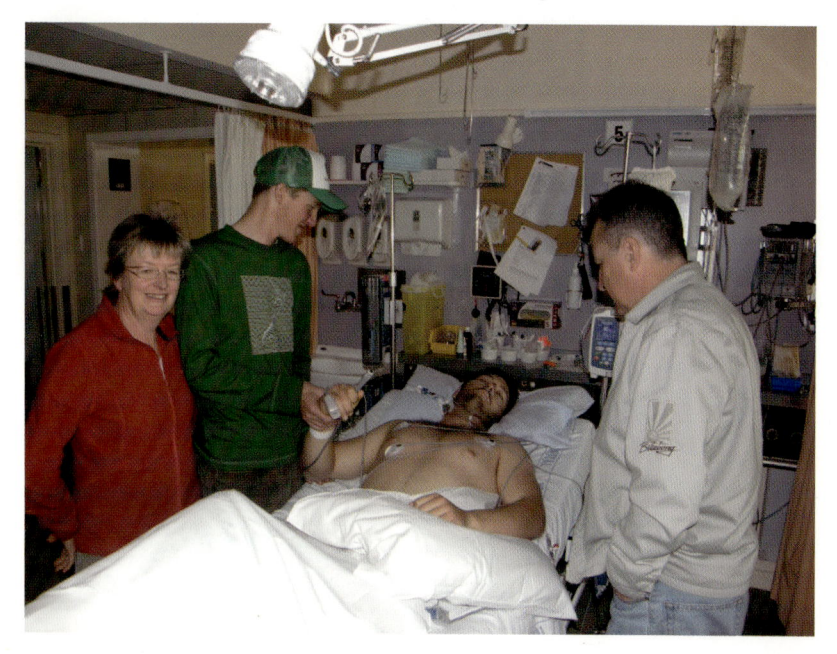

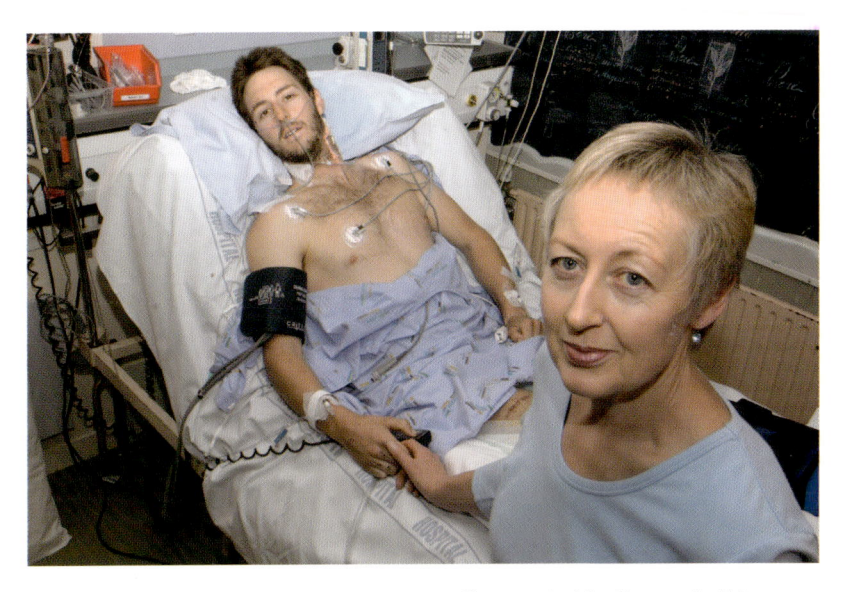

ABOVE: Mum holding my hand, hoping to offer a magical healing touch. Taken a few weeks later in the high dependency unit (HDU) when I was suffering from severe septicaemia (blood poisoning). PHOTO: WAIKATO DISTRICT HEALTH BOARD

BELOW: Aunty Linda, all the way from USA; me stretching my leg; and John Bonning – the emergency department doctor who saved my life.

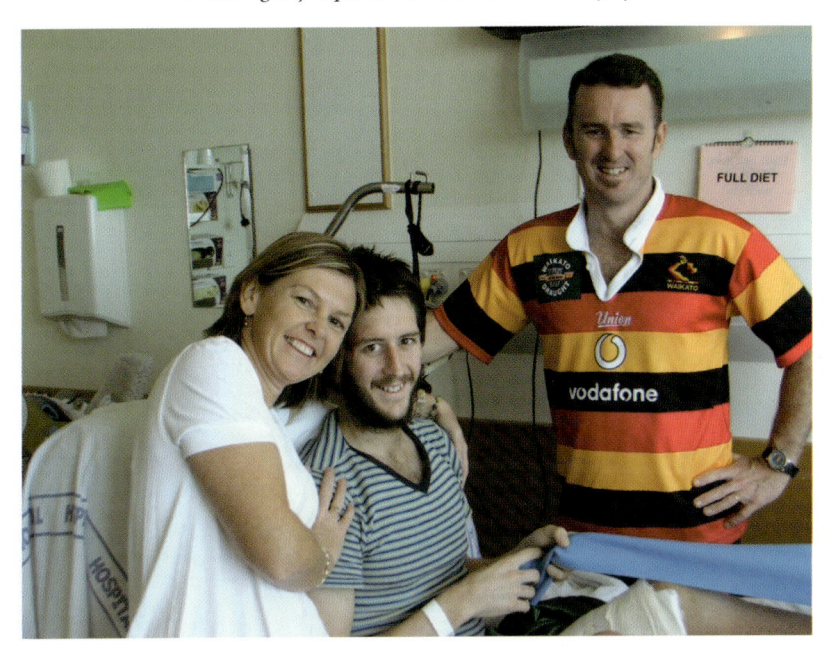

LEFT: Rock climbing with my new 'leg'.
PHOTO: BARRY PIKE

BELOW: My family and me outside the town hall in Auckland after I received my Honours (First Class) Degree. L–R: Uncle Ian, Grandad, Dad, Grandma, me, my brother, Mum and cousin Oliver.
PHOTO: JAMES CHRISTIE

was that he was a male. I did the OK? sign, then tapped with two fingers on my dive computer, which means, 'How much air do you have left?'

The diver replied with a solid 'OK'. Happy he was OK, I waved him on to continue diving with us. Diving solo is not recommended and any small problem could quickly turn into a deadly situation.

Ten minutes later, in a world of my own and absorbing the underwater beauty, I was disturbed by something tugging on my BCD. I spun around slowly, not knowing what to expect. It was the lonesome diver. His face appeared thirty centimetres from mine. He was in a panic, waving his dive computer in my face and reaching for my regulator in my mouth. The air gauge read 'zero psi' and was flashing.

He was putting me in danger by reaching for my regulator, so I punched at his hands to prevent him ripping the regulator out of my mouth. What on earth was this clown thinking as he ran out of air at a depth just above thirty metres, I thought to myself. This is ludicrous, he should have well over half a tank of air, just as Jesse and I did.

I acted quickly by moving out of the diver's reach, unclipping my second regulator and then handing it over to the now seriously panicking diver. After five or six breaths he seemed to calm down a little and was face to face with me, holding onto the shoulder straps of my BCD.

Then I saw him reach for his inflation device and press the inflation button that jetted air from his dive cylinder into his BCD. This would give him positive buoyancy and drag us too quickly towards the surface. I was horrified. Under no circumstances could we safely surface so quickly from such a depth. The microscopic air bubbles of nitrogen in our blood would quickly expand. This is similar to shaking up a bottle of Coke and unscrewing the lid too quickly. The bubbles in our blood, similar to those in the Coke bottle, would expand and bubble over. In a worst-case scenario, the bubbles could lodge in our hearts, lungs or brains causing almost certain death. This phenomenon is known as the bends, as it is more likely that a nitrogen bubble lodge in a joint – a shoulder, leg, knee or elbow. This is still very serious. It would require emergency evacuation to a decompression chamber. A decompression chamber is like a huge dive cylinder that people can fit into. Once someone is inside the chamber, it is pressurised (giving the same effect of pressure when diving at depth) to shrink the bubbles in the diver's blood, and then the pressure is very slowly decreased to the sea-level equivalent.

The lonesome diver, holding on to me for dear life, continued to drag me towards the surface. I grabbed his hand and pulled it from his inflation device. Then I dumped the air from both of our BCDs and furiously kicked with my fins. I thought about breaking his grip on my BCD, but then as we separated my spare regulator would rip from his mouth and he could drown. I was trying not to panic – it wasn't going to help the situation in any way whatsoever.

Kicking with as much effort as I could muster to get deeper, I finally stopped when I reached Jesse again. I wish I could have yelled at this guy! I made it clear through the harsh look in my eyes and by shaking my head that I was now in total control of the situation.

I made sure he had no air in his BCD and inflated my BCD to start ascending slowly. Concerned with the small amount of air remaining in my tank, which was now being consumed at twice its normal rate, I tried to slow my breathing. After several minutes we stopped at five metres for a three-minute safety stop. The safety stop would hopefully dissolve any remaining nitrogen bubbles in our blood.

Jesse had stuck with us the whole time without any trouble – until now. By the beam of his torch, I could see that Jesse had lost a fin and it was slowly sinking. It was now completely dark and I felt like we were pieces of space junk adrift for eternity. I waved my torch at Jesse to get his attention. I pointed at his fin with my torch. Jesse saw the fin straight away and descended like a wounded fish until he grabbed his fin. What else can go wrong now? I thought to myself.

I checked my dive watch and saw thirty seconds of the safety stop remaining.

A minute later the three of us broke the surface. I released my grip from the lonesome diver and as calmly as possible said, 'You could have killed the both of us, what the hell were you thinking? Did you not monitor your air?!'

'. . . Ahh . . . yeeeah . . . I did but . . . but it just ran out,' he spluttered.

I wasn't impressed.

We were now four or five hundred metres away from the boat. Jesse had told me that his fin strap had broken and he couldn't swim back. I waved my torch above my head from side to side – the international sign for help. Soon the skipper was bouncing through the darkness in a small inflatable boat to pick the three of us up.

Back aboard, the diver apologised for causing a panic and explained how he had lost his dive buddy. I told him that he should have surfaced immediately and found his buddy. The drive home was a sobering reminder of how quickly things can go wrong. Jesse and I talked about how important it is to always be with another person when in the water, especially when diving. We agreed that we had learnt a lesson tonight; keep an eye on each other's air more often and, if separated underwater, follow the recommended procedure of surfacing immediately.

CHAPTER SEVEN

MIGHTIER THAN A MOUNTAIN

*I know a man mightier than a mountain.
So if I'm moaning again that my pencil lacks
lead or my belly needs bread, remind me,
there's a man mightier than a mountain.
If I slump in self-sorrow or squabble,
tomorrow remind me,
there's a man mightier than a mountain.
Should I break down and cry or let out a sigh
that morning's arrived, remind me,
there's a man mightier than a mountain.
And when I praise Hillary as a mountain-man
or Meads as a mountain-man, remind me,
of William Pike.
A man mightier than a mountain.*
ANDREW WHITSON (WHITTY)

(Whitty is a friend of mine who went to Westlake Boys High School with me. When he heard of my accident, he sat down, put his extremely creative brain into use and came up with this astonishing poem. My mum first read it to me in hospital. It is the most tear-jerking thing I have ever heard.)

As quickly as the frigid water engulfed me from head to toe, it was gone. It was like I was in the bath and the plug had been pulled out – the water just disappeared. Right then, in that instant, I honestly thought, without a word of a lie, that I was going to die.

I could hear James screaming in fear, saying, 'What is happening?! What is happening?!'

I was unable to give James an answer. I was grunting under my breath, trying to free myself from the mess I was in.

After a few seconds I felt that some luck was on my side, I wasn't going to drown. I didn't have time to appreciate my luck, as I felt a mixture of mild pain and pressure on my legs begin to set in.

In a frightened voice James kept repeating, 'What the hell just happened?!'

I was in disbelief, but I was positive that the mountain had just erupted.

'The mountain has just erupted, the mountain erupted,' was my only answer for James.

I calmly pleaded, 'Help me, help me, James, I'm stuck and can't get my legs out.'

James replied, 'OK, OK, hold on, I'm coming.'

Still in a calm voice, I said, 'Let's get my legs out, I think my foot is dislocated. Let's get it out and get down the mountain.'

I was focused and determined to get down the mountain. I kept repeating, 'We're going to get through this, we're going to get through this.'

In the dark, I tried to come to terms with what had just happened, but I quickly realised there wasn't time for this. Immediately I knew I had to keep focused and deal with one problem at a time. I wasn't scared at this stage, I just felt a sense of urgency to free myself.

Before I had time to act, James's headlamp broke the darkness and he approached me, walking over the sharp frozen debris in socks and dressed in only a lightweight polypropylene top, Swanndri, and long pants. He was already shivering. It seemed that the moment I saw James shivering, I began to shiver too. Perhaps so much was going on, my body was dealing with other things and forgot its natural defence to the cold.

James's headlamp now shone directly on me as he surveyed my frightening situation. For the first time I was able to take a mental note of the position I had been forced into. I was in a sitting position with a thirty centimetre gap between my back and the right-hand side of the door frame. My upper right thigh and femur were at a right angle to my upper body and my knee bent at ninety degrees before disappearing abruptly into the jumble of rocks, mud, snow, ice and splinters of wood. My left leg was in a similar position, except for my knee. The leg extended at a smaller angle, perhaps forty-five degrees, before disappearing into the jumble of debris. I had no doubt in my mind that I would be able to free myself. I thought as soon as James could help me, we'd be able to free my legs – no sweat.

All of a sudden my vision blurred and I began to see black spots clouding my eyes. I confessed to James, 'I'm going to faint James, I'm going to faint.'

I felt I was slipping away. Slipping away to where? I wasn't sure – perhaps death? I felt a desperate urge to say something in case they were the last words I would ever say.

I managed to say, 'I've had a wicked day's climbing, I saw a nice sunset, tell my family I love them.'

I began to fall backwards to my right and into the door frame. As I finished my sentence I only just managed to make out the next thing that happened. James obviously wasn't going to let me faint, and he slapped me firmly across the face. It made a sharp slapping noise and I instantly bolted upright again. It worked. James literally slapped me back to reality and I began to focus on freeing myself again.

As fast as I could, I started to pick up small rocks and throw them in any direction, away from my legs. I soon became frustrated that I wasn't making any progress.

I tried to move the rocks from around my right leg with my frozen hands. James began to dig around my left leg, scraping away at mud, rocks and bits of wood smashed off the door frame. I could feel some movement in my left leg but nothing in my right leg. I changed my mind and decided to help James free my left leg.

Seconds later I felt confident that my left leg would come free. I was relieved when James tugged my left leg out from underneath some rocks at an awkward angle. A huge sense of relief overcame me.

A brief inspection of my left leg showed no major injury, although I was concerned about the effort it took to straighten and contract my leg. I thought that there was something wrong with my knee, maybe it was broken or dislocated, I wasn't sure. This was a small, irrelevant problem and I focused my mind on freeing my right leg.

I heard James ask me again, 'What just happened?'

'It erupted,' I said.

James didn't reply, as he was devoted to freeing my right leg. I could see he wasn't making any progress with his hands. Thinking of an alternative, James said, 'I'll pull you out from under your shoulders, OK?'

I was prepared to try anything and said, 'Yeah, all right, give that a go.'

I felt James reach under my armpits with his hands and strain as he lifted me. In immense pain I yelled, 'ARGGHHH! My leg, my leg. The bones in my leg are grating against each other when you do that!'

It felt like I was dunking my leg in and out of a red-hot cauldron of magma.

'All right, I'll keep digging then,' James said.

I could see James's hands wriggling further than before down the front of my right leg.

'I can see some blood,' he said.

'Don't worry,' I replied. 'Oh, what colour is it?' I added.

'It's bright red.'

That wasn't what I wanted to hear. I was sure that meant an artery had been severed, releasing bright red blood that had been recently oxygenated by my heart. It wasn't good news. It had crossed my mind earlier that I could be losing vast quantities of blood from my leg, which was covered by rocks, mud and water. For some reason I couldn't think of anything to stop the bleeding.

Surely there must be a solution, I thought.

Following more efforts from James and I digging around my right leg, I could see that we weren't achieving what we wanted. Our hands began to burn from the terrible cold. They stopped functioning, becoming useless, lifeless, redundant bits of meat.

'I can't use my hands anymore, I'll get the shovel,' said James.

In a now desperate attempt to free my leg with my useless hands, I persisted pathetically in trying to dig out any rocks with my hands, but they were just not working.

Within seconds James stood before me with a brown metal shovel in his hands. The shovel belonged to the Dome Shelter and was stronger than our aluminium and plastic shovels. James jammed the spade underneath the debris. I think he managed to shift some rocks after a few attempts. 'Move back,' James said as he forced the shovel somewhere in between a rock and my leg.

I could see him leaning on the shovel with all his weight, trying to make progress in freeing my right leg. I was beginning to feel that every method we tried to free my right leg was failing. I shut those negative thoughts out from my head and tried to think positively and rationally, for I was so stubbornly determined to free myself.

Soon James said what I was hoping he wouldn't say. 'It's not working either. The shovel . . . '

'OK, try an ice axe then,' I said.

I immediately began to use my hands again to free my leg. I found it hard to comprehend that my hands could not and would not free me. I just felt like I had to do *something* to free myself. If I didn't keep trying I felt guilty that I wasn't doing all I could to get free.

Out of nowhere James began swinging an ice axe at the rocks surrounding my right leg. Using all his strength to bash the stubborn rocks, in mid-swing he sternly commanded, 'Look out or you'll lose a finger.'

My fingers were dangerously close to where James was swinging the ice axe. Once again I couldn't help my hands from wandering around my right leg. Again, I felt I had to be trying to free myself, no matter what. I told myself I would never give up.

Bright orange sparks lit up the dark room for a split second as the ice axe struck the rocks next to my leg. To our disappointment, the sparks were the only result from James's huge effort. A feeling of utter desperation washed over me, as nothing had moved the rocks, no matter how hard we tried.

For about ten minutes I was still in the same sitting position I had been forced into. For no reason I began to talk nonsense. Thinking that I knew exactly what I was saying and that it was the best idea, I said to James, 'It's not working, go hide in the escape hatch and we'll wait until help in the morning.'

I don't know why, maybe a combination of hypothermia, blood loss and shock, but my thinking became irrational and my comments senseless.

Using his functional common sense and rational thinking, James strongly opposed my irrational comment.

'No way! I'm going to go down the mountain for help.'

Seconds later it occurred to me that it wasn't a bad idea. In fact, I knew it was the one and only way we'd get help to free my right leg.

Knowing that there wasn't a second to spare, James had a brief but frantic look around the shelter.

'What do I do?'

His question struck me hard and I remembered it was his first time on Mt Ruapehu. What if James got lost on the way to find help?

Thinking rationally again, I said, 'Get your boots, get an ice axe, crampons and a jacket, and just go for help – try to reach the New Zealand Alpine Club hut.'

James began ferreting through the debris in search of anything that could help him or me. On the ladder leading up into the escape hatch were James's boots.

What on earth would he have done if his boots were buried? Either he wouldn't have gone down the mountain for help or else he would have almost certainly suffered serious frostbite to both his feet.

James grabbed his boots, slipped them on and did a rough job in tying up the laces. I hadn't realised that I was wearing my jacket – which James had put on me earlier – until James said, 'Give me your jacket, I can't find mine.'

Without delay I surrendered my jacket to James. My jacket had protected me slightly from the gentle -15°C windchill that I was now fully exposed to. I knew if James didn't get down the mountain safely, I would surely die – with or without my jacket on.

James started firing me some items of gear. It felt like all my Christmases had come at once. He threw my sodden down jacket at me; I struggled a little and managed to put it on. I was unable to zip it up because my hands were not functioning in the extreme cold. Next my headlamp landed on top of some mud and rocks in front of me. I turned it on – it worked! I put it on my head. At least when James left the hut I wouldn't be in total darkness.

I didn't know what to say when James handed me our two cell phones.

'Here – call 111.'

I thought it was too good to be true – and it was. I held James's cell phone in my hand. It was vibrating non-stop, most likely from being soaked with water. I pushed a few buttons and nothing happened; the phone's screen was frozen. I threw it into the corner of the shelter, not because I was angry but because I had never trusted cell phones to work in the outdoors and I was so right – it was useless. I picked up my cell phone, hoping for a miracle, but it was no different from James's. I threw it into the corner of the shelter too.

I knew that I was in a life-threatening situation and it was slowly getting worse. I was concerned for James too, but there was absolutely nothing I could do to help him. I couldn't believe the situation we were in. It was crazy.

The situation seemed to get more real and feel more like it was actually happening when I said to James, 'Can you get me warm? Find me some clothes or something? Can you put a boot on my left foot?'

James unhooked his waterproof/windproof pants from the wall and put them around my neck. From somewhere he whipped out his sleeping bag and gave it to me, saying, 'Here, use my bag, put it around you or something.'

There was silence as he looked for my boots. I stared at my left foot. It looked OK but I couldn't feel it. I thought it was because of the cold. That bothered me and I was worried about frostbite.

James finished searching for my boots and came back to

me saying, 'I can't find your boots, they must be underneath the rocks or something. Sorry.'

The next few things that happened are etched into my memory and until this day I can picture them in my head, crystal clear. James was standing in front of me with his boots on, an ice axe in his hand and his headlamp turned on. He was wearing thin polypropylene gloves and my orange jacket. When I saw his ice axe, I knew I could use its leash as a tourniquet.

'Give me your ice axe leash and help me make a tourniquet.'

James hurriedly unthreaded the leash from his ice axe and assisted me in putting it around my thigh, above my right knee.

I pointed at a piece of wood and said, 'That wood, give me that piece of wood. I'll use it to tighten the leash.'

James handed me the wood, which was about the size of a thirty-centimetre ruler, only a bit thicker. I fed it through the two loops on the end of the leash and twisted it around and around until I was sure the blood flow would be stopped by the tourniquet.

James reached over my head and grabbed my GPS, which was hanging from a hook on the wall, then put its lanyard around his wrist. He had a look of worry and uncertainty on his face as he said, 'OK, I'm going to go now, I'll be back soon, you'll be OK.'

James uneasily walked a few steps across the rubble with his back to me. He turned around and looked at me.

My last words to James were, 'Tell my mum and dad I love them.'

'Nah, mate, you can tell them that yourself,' he replied.

And then James was gone. I was left sitting in the Dome Shelter, seriously cold, crushed and severely injured, and now all alone.

It was so quiet – almost so quiet that it hurt my ears. I noticed my breathing was rapid. I think I was hyperventilating. I tried to take deep breaths and calm myself down but I couldn't.

I thought to myself, OK, it's just me now. I need to calm down and take some deep breaths. I couldn't stop myself shivering. I was shivering so much my whole body was shaking. I could taste the revolting tang of sulphur in my mouth. I spat a few times onto the debris in front of me to clear my mouth. Then my headlamp cut out. It just stopped working. So I threw it into the corner of the shelter, next to the cell phones.

Sitting awkwardly and staring out the door I thought I heard another small rumble from the crater lake.

I'm a goner if it blows again, I thought to myself.

Looking out the main door into the night, I could see that the discoloured snow was well lit up by the light of the full moon. Bits of wood were dangling from the demolished door frame, and with the moon's light they cast freaky shadows inside the shelter.

I could feel the bone-numbing wind on my face, which gave me an idea. I pulled James's sleeping bag over my head, kind of like a big sock. I crossed my arms and tucked my numb hands under my armpits. I was well aware my breathing was rapid and shallow – it wasn't good. I knew I was experiencing shock and needed urgent medical attention.

I was lucky that my first aid knowledge was pretty advanced. I had recently completed an outdoor first aid course. I had two St John Ambulance first aid certificates – level one and level two. I had read widely on first aid in the outdoors. I had done enough mountaineering, tramping and surf lifesaving over the years to know the extreme danger of hypothermia. I knew each stage of hypothermia, what it would do to my body, what would happen and when I was most likely to die.

From now on there would be no surprises. I didn't rate my chances of surviving my situation very highly at all. I was pretty sure I would die here. I knew the track my body would go down until, ultimately, my death. I knew hypothermia would slowly send me to sleep and I would never wake up again.

I wanted to stay awake and keep my mind active. I began calculations in my head of when James might arrive at the NZAC hut and when rescuers might get to me. I tried to think realistically and knew I needed a miracle to survive and it would take another miracle for that miracle to happen.

I began thinking: It took us two and a half hours to get from the NZAC hut to the Dome Shelter. If James doesn't get hurt or lost on the way down he might reach the hut in one and a half to two hours. James will probably get lost, I don't know how he'll find the hut in the dark. Damn. That'll be around 10.30 p.m. or 11 p.m. It will take at least two hours for a rescue team to be notified, get geared up, and somehow get up the mountain. That's if they come up, they might be worried about more eruptions. That makes it 1 a.m. or 1.30 a.m. If they walk up from the top of Bruce Road then it'll take them at least four or five hours and I'll be dead by then. If they use a helicopter then maybe they'll be here by 2 a.m. or 2.30 a.m. at the earliest. It's 9 p.m. now, so I'll be dead in maybe four or five hours max, that's if I don't bleed to death first. If a rescue team can get to me before 2 a.m. then my chances of survival might be twenty per cent. My chances of surviving until sunrise will be zero per cent.

Having calculated my chances of surviving, it didn't surprise me that I could be dead soon. Before I completely accepted that I was going to die, I needed to try and get my leg out. I figured if I got it out, and I could slide down the mountain on my bum, somehow I'd get there.

I pulled James's sleeping bag off my head and lay it next

to me. I instantly felt the cold air attacking my face and upper body again but I needed to take it off anyway, as it was getting difficult to breathe in there.

I took a few deep breaths, placed my hands palm down on the rocks underneath me and pushed down to lift myself up off the ground. I knew it would hurt but I didn't care. I pushed as hard as I could with my hands and tried to pull my leg out. I screamed like a little girl with the pain. It was so intense, it felt like my leg was on fire. Each time I tried to yank my leg out, I felt faint as the broken bones noisily grated together and the black spots impaired my vision.

I wasn't going to accept that I couldn't get my leg out until I had tried everything possible to free it. I tried pulling my leg out three more times. After that I accepted there was no way I could get it out. I was buggered.

Out of options, I thought seriously and carefully about cutting my leg off. I was going to weigh up the positive and negatives but realised I had nothing sharp enough to do the job. Also, it would take a hell of a lot of effort to break my femur and I would surely bleed to death. I did think of cutting my leg from the knee joint, avoiding having to break bones and only cutting tendons. Still, I didn't have anything sharp enough to do the job, and it wouldn't have stopped the onset of hypothermia, so I forgot about that idea.

I continued to shiver violently and uncontrollably. I knew shivering was my body's natural reaction to the cold – to try and warm it up by moving – so I welcomed the shivering. If someone had been watching me they'd have thought I was being electrocuted, with the amount of shivering I was doing.

James's sleeping bag was still lying where I left it. I pulled it over my head again, crossed my arms, tucked my hands under my armpits and thought of ways to raise my body temperature. Every time I exhaled I could feel the warmth in my breath fill the small space enclosed by James's sleeping bag, and making it feel ever so slightly warmer, but I doubt it would have raised my body temperature.

My bum started to burn from the cold and the uncomfortable debris I was sitting on. In search of a solution I looked over my right shoulder and saw my shredded sleeping mat in the room behind me. I was startled at the sight of my sleeping mat completely shredded to bits. It made me feel sick at the thought of the force needed to do that. If I could slide it under my bum I would be more comfortable, and the cold from the debris wouldn't be able to transfer to my bum.

Despite the pain that grew worse each time I moved a centimetre, I leant back through the door to my right side and reached a piece of my sleeping mat. I felt the bones in my right leg moving and grating against each other. My right hand was barely able to pick up the sleeping mat. Somehow I closed all of my fingers together at once and grasped the sleeping mat against my palm. I dragged it closer to me and managed to slide it under my bum, causing horrendous pain in my right leg.

My bum was more comfortable now and didn't feel as cold as before; that was a bonus. Overall I was sitting in an awkward and painful position with little chance of getting comfortable. I began to experience lower-back pain from slouching forwards over my legs. The thirty-centimetre gap between my back and the door frame also aggravated my lower back when I leaned back onto the door frame for a change in position and a small triangular gap was created where my bum met the floor. Although the pain from my crushed right leg was like nothing I had ever felt before, my lower-back pain was really starting to bother me. Whatever position I changed to, I couldn't get my back comfortable. It seems silly that I was concerned about minuscule muscle soreness in my back when my right leg was squashed flat as a pancake, but that's how it was.

I tried to ignore my back pain and stared into the pitch darkness. I wasn't feeling as cold as I had been some time ago. That worried me as it meant that hypothermia had me firmly in its lethal grip. I tried thinking of other ways to warm myself, but there was nothing.

I sat quietly in the -8°C air temperature and listened to the panting of my rapid breathing. I began to think about how I wanted to live my life, not how it would end.

I thought: I don't want to die like this, not here, not now, I'm too young. I want to accomplish so much more in my life. I want to explore mountain ranges all over the world. I want to go where few people have ever been, see what few people have ever seen. I want to teach children, fill them with knowledge, offer them rich experiences, make them happy and make them love life. I want to spend hours chatting to my family and friends. I want to see them, touch them and hear them laughing. I want to hear myself laughing. I want to find a lovely wife, have children, watch them grow up, spend lots of time with them and show them the great outdoors. I want to hold my children, comfort them in times of need, watch them grow up, and be at their twenty-first birthday parties surrounded by all their mates and our family. I want to die a happy old man, completely satisfied with my journey through life, with no regrets.

That was how I wanted to live my life. I didn't want it to be cut short. It wasn't fair; I felt that I was being robbed of my one and only special chance of experiencing life.

When thinking about all the things I wanted to experience in life, I could feel my body beginning to slow down, creeping closer and closer to death. I couldn't move my hands or my left leg anymore – they were completely numb. I was slumped over inside James's sleeping bag. I felt more comfortable as the seconds ticked by. I had forgotten about the tourniquet on my leg. Even if I had remembered to keep it tight, I wouldn't have been able to, because my hands weren't working. The pain in my right leg seemed to have settled down a bit. My breathing rate slowed a little but was still quite quick, about one breath a second.

Still breathing and still alive, I decided I wasn't going to give up without a gruelling fight. Even with the odds stacked highly against me, I was committed to surviving. I held onto my strong desire for how I wanted to live my life and the things I had yet to accomplish. I thought of my family and my friends. I wondered how they would react as the news of my death was broken to them. I thought about their tears of sadness and how difficult it would be for them to accept the tragic way I had died. I didn't want my family and friends to go through a terrible time of grieving over my death. I said to myself, 'Stay awake, be strong and I'll get through this.'

I tried to flood my head with positive thoughts but no matter what I did, said, or thought, nothing would change the situation I was in. I understood that I couldn't do anything about my situation. I just hoped for the best – that was all I could do. While waiting for help, there was not one moment when I began to feel angry, sad or frustrated. I lay calmly on my side in the cold and in pain. If I died, I died. I accepted that because I couldn't change it.

At one stage I thought about how lucky I was not to have any regrets. I felt pleased that I had taken every opportunity possible to spend time with family and friends, go tramping, mountaineering, scuba diving, cycling, surf lifesaving and much more. I felt I had made the most of every opportunity to see, be with and have fun with my family and friends. Not one thing entered my mind that made me think, Gee, I wish I had done more of that.

I was 110 per cent satisfied that I had made the most

of every moment and lived a full life of varied experiences, amazing adventures and fun times.

Thinking about how I had no regrets is the last thing I can remember about waiting for help in the Dome Shelter. I can't pinpoint the exact time or the thoughts that were in my head as I drifted off to sleep and into a coma. I can remember squinting at my watch, but I couldn't make out the time, despite the fact it has glow-in-the-dark hands. Perhaps that was about when my brain stopped functioning normally. I can remember lying on my left side, not thinking about the cold and feeling OK. I wasn't in much pain, and, strangely, I almost felt happy. I have put the feeling of happiness down to the severe hypothermia my body was experiencing.

At a guess, I thought the eruption had happened just after 8 p.m. I thought that James was with me for fifteen minutes or less before he went for help, and that he had been gone for an hour before I drifted into a coma.

Thinking back now to when I was unconscious, I feel that I experienced what it must be like to be dead. It was strange. It felt like nothing. No thoughts, no emotions, no dreaming, no feelings – no connection to the outside world. Nothing.

It was as though my mind went completely blank, lost in a black hole in space. I guess that when people think of something going completely blank they think of the colour black or white. I didn't see black or white. I didn't see anything – zero, zilch, nada. In a weird way, I feel very privileged to have had the chance to be as close as you can get to dying, remembering everything that happened, without actually dying.

CHAPTER EIGHT

WORDS FROM OTHERS: THE COLD HARD FACTS

Success seems to be largely a matter of hanging on after others have let go.
WILLIAM FEATHER

This chapter is almost entirely written by other people. I had no idea about what was happening while I was unconscious in the Dome Shelter. Facts that I have rewritten in my own words have been sourced from my parents, doctors and medical notes.

To give a complete understanding of what happened in between the Dome Shelter and hospital, people that played an important part in my survival have written their own accounts of what happened after 8.30 p.m. on 25 September, 2007.

As I drifted off into a coma, James began running down the Whakapapa Glacier in a desperate plea for help. James has written about the events that unfolded in front of his eyes:

'Tell my parents and family I love them,' I heard William say.

Without thinking too much, I replied, 'Nah, mate, you can tell them yourself.'

I didn't bother with goodbyes or saying anything about where I was going. I knew I was going to be seeing him again soon, even though I hadn't really worked out what I was doing!

Instantly the whole surrounding environment had changed. It had gone from a pure white colour to a black and grey mess. The surface of the snow looked like the moon. There were craters from rock bombs everywhere, some only a few centimetres deep, some over half a metre deep. It was weird. I didn't even look at the crater lake, I looked straight towards the glacier. That was north, the direction I figured the New Zealand Alpine Club hut to be in. If I was wrong I knew that eventually I would meet civilisation somewhere.

The glacier didn't look right though; there was what looked like a black river running as far as I could see (which wasn't that far). For a second I remembered what William had said about the mountain erupting – if it had erupted then it could well be quite hot down there. That was the last time I had that thought. I started bounding down the side of the Dome towards the Whakapapa Glacier. It was tough work. I was jumping into the craters left by lava bombs, kind of using them like a staircase, because without crampons the ice was really slippery. Once on the glacier, where it was not as steep, I was able to pick up my pace.

There was one thought going through my mind as I was running and it made me move pretty quick: I have to get help.

On the steeper parts of the glacier where I had to slow my running I tried bum-sliding. The only problem was that I only had long johns on – a rather thin layer between the ice and my skin – and they created friction as I slid, which soon began to burn. Needless to say, the bum-sliding didn't last very long at all.

Soon I was running again, and this time the slope

was easing out, so I could go faster. It was still very tricky though. I had to dodge rocks and small craters, which I could only really see as I was placing my feet. I was worried about twisting an ankle or falling and hurting myself – I certainly couldn't afford to do that. I kept on going at full speed. After I had been running for maybe ten minutes I noticed that the glacier started veering away from where I wanted to go. I had to make a decision to leave the glacier and try and find my own way down the mountain. I didn't like this idea; following the glacier was easy, as it wasn't a steep slope and it was heading in the right direction. With the lahar following the same path, it seemed like a safe route down. I had to find something else to help guide me down the mountain.

Ski tracks – perfect! Several skiers had come to the crater lake via the glacier so they must have left tracks somewhere. All I had to do was find them – and find them I did. I was back in my comfort zone again, following a path I was sure would lead to civilisation, to help for William.

In the distance there was this light; it didn't seem right, as it was too high for it to be on this part of the mountain. I yelled more or less for the sake of it. The light didn't seem to notice me. Stuff it. I have to keep going. The light seemed too far out of my way, with too little signs of help, for me to bother with it.

But suddenly there was more light, lots of light, so much light that I was casting a shadow. I knew what that light was, too. William and I had seen these yesterday; they were the lights of the snowcats, which spend hours every night grooming the ski fields for the next day's skiers.

Immediately I changed my plan. This guy wasn't really that far away.

I shouted really loud.

'Help! Help! My mate's pinned.'

A voice replied, 'Hello?'

'Help! Help! My mate's pinned,' I yelled again and I started running towards the voice.

'Be careful! The lahar could still be moving.'

I had to get across the lahar to get to him but I didn't care if I had to walk across fire; I wanted to talk to him really bad.

Judging by the light, I was able to work out exactly where he was. The glacier had created a sort of gully, and initially I was running down through the bottom of it, but I had turned out of it and up the eastern side. He was perched on the western side at the top of a chairlift – the Far West T Bar.

I went straight up to him and rattled off like a chainsaw, saying something about my mate William Pike's leg being stuck in the Dome Shelter at the top of the mountain. I probably had to repeat it a few times because I was in such a rush to get things happening. I didn't know it yet but he had also been through a rather close ordeal as well. He was already on his radio when I turned up. He was now talking with a whole bunch of people about sorting out a rescue.

As he was talking I was madly trying to give him the details about William, catch my breath and calm myself down all at the same time.

I was now virtually useless. I was only just starting to work out how cold it was, and I was shaking madly. During my trot down the mountain I had collected a lot of snow in my boots and my feet were well numb.

I think I got a 'my name's Shane, by the way', in between our frantic discussions with Search and Rescue.

He invited me into his snowcat because 'it was warmer in there.'

I was stoked – more because it was a cool looking machine than because I needed to get warm!

I took off William's jacket, turned it inside out and laid it on the seat. The snowcat was immaculate inside and I didn't want to dirty the thing!

Then I heard what had just happened to Shane. He had been grooming a steeper ski field and had his snowcat attached by a steel cable to an anchor at the top of the run. He had been on his way back up the ski field with the sweeper – the bit that smoothes out the snow on the back of the snowcat – raised.

Out of the corner of his eye he saw this wall of black stuff coming at him, probably a few metres high and at least ten metres across. Shane had been around and had seen the lahars Mt Ruapehu produced in 1996. He said that he barely needed to think to realise that he had to move – and fast.

His foot was on the floor and he red-lined the poor snowcat straight up the run. The lahar missed his snowcat by about a metre. I was starting to realise how lucky I was that he was here.

We talked about a few things to calm each other down. We discussed the All Blacks and how they might perform in the World Cup, then he said, 'You don't have girlfriends or wives or anything stupid like that do you?'

I laughed. William and I had earlier discussed how easy life was at the moment without having the drama that a girlfriend might cause!

I think after the shock of almost being taken out by a lahar flying down the mountain, seeing a guy come down the mountain in long johns and a Swanndri must have been a lot for Shane to comprehend.

Shane also mentioned that he only saw me because of the light of my headlamp. I'd forgotten I'd even worn it on the way down. If I hadn't had it on or it hadn't been working, I would probably still have been running.

Shane was constantly on the radio – he had two actually,

a little hand-held one and the CB radio in the snowcat. Both were going mad as he was explaining what had happened where, how bad it was and all the rest. It was about this time that I started swaying in the seat – hoping that William was going to be all right. I was sure he was going to be fine but I had completely lost track of time and could not work out how long I had been gone for. The smell and taste of sulphur started to freak me out. It was everywhere. The smell started to fill the cabin of the snowcat. It was not pleasant.

After about twenty minutes we saw the light of another snowcat come up over the ridge. It was here to help us out. The driver spent about five minutes carving a makeshift path for us to follow so we could get out of the danger zone.

Soon we were out of the way of the lahar and Shane got out to talk to the other snowcat crew about his evening's excitement. Then we were back on our way down the mountain. I reckon Shane had his foot on the floor again. It was great too – those snowcats can really move and they don't let any amount of snow slow them down.

I worked out that if I hadn't met Shane when and where I did, it would have taken me a long time to get to civilisation and any form of rescue.

We arrived outside the Ruapehu Alpine Rescue Organisation headquarters and a man came out to talk to me. He asked how William was when I left him, what had jammed his leg and how they might be able to free him.

'An angle grinder – it's like concrete.'

I couldn't think of any other tool that would be able to free his leg. What a stupid thing to say . . . why would they have an angle grinder? How on earth would it work at the top of a mountain with no electricity?

I told the guy where William was and asked if he knew of the shelter. He knew it all right. He'd been there lots of times. I was comforted by that. William would be OK, I thought.

Shane and I were once again off in the snowcat. We went to Iwikau village (on the Whakapapa ski field), where I was given the opportunity to swap my smelly, wet, cold thermals and Swanndri for some warm, dry clothes and a few biscuits to help get rid of the gross taste in my mouth.

There I met Constable Conrad Smith of the National Park police station. He took me and my rubbish bag of smelly clothes in his four-by-four to the DOC area office. It was the same office where only a day earlier William and I had been filling in our intentions forms and checking the weather forecasts.

A DOC area manager, Bhrent Guy, was there for the questioning process. I could hardly believe what I was saying as I told Constable Smith about what had just happened.

Constable Smith kept telling me that I was going to have to ring my parents. I kept telling him that I would rather he did it. In the end, he managed to convince me that it would be best if I did it. I could see I was going to have difficulty explaining this one. Almost every time William and I decide to go on a mission or go adventuring, we come back with interesting tales about how some crazy thing had happened. This time it was a little more extreme than usual.

Before I rang my parents, Constable Smith went out of the room with his radio. He came back in and said that the rescue team had brought William down off the mountain.

'He's a status one and it could go either way.'

I decided not to believe him. When I left William he wasn't that bad, considering our sleep had been interrupted by an eruption, so I was convinced he would be OK in the end.

I was given a phone. I had to ring Mum and Dad. Great. I dialled the number. The phone in their bedroom is on

Mum's side of the bed. I figured I'd better talk to Dad. He might take it a little better than Mum.

'Hi Mum, it's James. Can I speak to Dad please?'

'OK.'

You could tell she couldn't work out what was happening. There was no way I should have been calling but she was clearly half asleep.

'Hi Dad, it's James. You know how William and I are staying on Mt Ruapehu tonight?'

'Yes.'

'And you know how it's a volcano?'

'Yes.'

'Ah, well, it's just erupted.'

That was about as clear as I could make it while trying to be calm about the whole thing. I explained that I was fine but William was still stuck up there but help was on the way. That was it. Way to freak your parents out!

Constable Smith sorted out a room for me to stay in at the Chateau Tongariro. I had always wanted to stay there; it's an iconic and rather famous hotel. Unfortunately I was too out of it to take it all in at the time.

I arrived in my room and was back on the phone to Mum and Dad. I explained the story in a little more detail and they said they'd be down mid-morning. Somehow I knew I couldn't wait that long. I'm a family person and like my family around me in difficult situations. I wanted them here now. I knew Mum wouldn't sleep either.

After about an hour of thinking, they packed the car and started to drive down. After all, I was stuck down here: my car might have been in the car park across the road but my keys were at the top of the mountain.

I spent probably a total of two hours bathing and showering, just trying to eradicate the sulphur taste and smell from my body. It was starting to almost haunt me.

By 2 a.m. I was lying in bed staring at the ceiling. I wasn't going to be able to sleep no matter how hard I tried. I couldn't close my eyes. I was sure that if I did, something would happen and I would be in a dire situation again. It was annoyingly quiet as well. Every time I heard the slightest noise, I thought the mountain was erupting again. It's fair to say I was freaked out.

I had the TV on but wasn't really watching or listening to it. After a painful five hours the seven o'clock news started. I've never liked people who try and tell you something without knowing all the facts and this news guy was one of those people. The idiot was feeling sorry that the ski field had been closed on such an awesome day for skiing. If he had just known half of what had happened up there he wouldn't have been so cavalier about it.

Eventually bulletins, although mostly incorrect, started talking about a climber who had been at the top of the mountain when it had erupted. They said he had a severely injured leg and hypothermia. That made sense. It was pretty cold up there and I could feel the bone sticking out the front of William's leg, so of course the injury was severe!

At about 8.30 a.m. my parents arrived, and it was really good to see them. Dad couldn't get over how bad I smelt and he made sure I knew it. Good on you, Dad!

We departed the Chateau, whose staff kindly didn't charge me for my wakeful night, and walked the fifty metres to the DOC office. There were lots of television crews around and lots of people trying to get noticed.

Inside the DOC office we met with a lady who had been involved with a helicopter accident at the top of Mt Ruapehu a year earlier. She warned us of how nasty the media could be. To be honest I found it hard to believe they were here – this was just another of William and James's crazy adventure tales as far as I was concerned.

WORDS FROM OTHERS: THE COLD HARD FACTS

After sawing the steering-wheel lock off my car, we departed Mt Ruapehu for Waikato Hospital. I was feeling a little better so I told Mum I wanted to drive, even though I was tired. I just wanted to keep myself occupied. We stopped in Taupo and had Burger King for lunch. I realised then that I hadn't had any food in a very long time.

Eventually we arrived at Waikato Hospital. I still wasn't really fazed. I half expected to stroll into a room and have a chat to William about when we would be heading back to the mountain to finish our trip. That was a little naïve. William was in intensive care – sweet as, though – he was still going to be all right.

Suddenly, as we were exiting the elevator on the third floor, it hit me. It was as if the mood or feeling of the place had just slammed into me. My head dropped and I felt weird. It just wasn't right. There were people everywhere; I didn't want to see people. I couldn't believe what I had just been through and I certainly didn't want to be telling other people about my ordeal. I needed to internalise it myself first.

Mum and Dad led me to William's parents, Barry and Tracy. The people here knew my name. I recognised a few faces – they were William's mates and there were a fair few of them. Barry and Tracy greeted me. They didn't look great.

Barry took me into a small room where a couple of William's mates were sitting down. He sat me on a chair and explained the situation. He told me that William had lost a leg. I'm not sure how much else I took in but the general atmosphere of the place made me feel down. I sort of explained a little bit about what had happened and then was told I could go in with Barry and see William.

Intensive care was a grim place – most, if not all, of the machines are more alive than the patients in there. William was one of those patients. There were tubes and machines and things stuck all over him. This was not how he was meant to be.

I was hit by something again. I had left William in a condition I figured wasn't too bad, considering what had happened, and now he was like this. Something must have happened while I was gone. Cold happened. When cold happens, and it happens on this level, it's tough. I held William's hand. It wasn't that warm and I wasn't allowed to move it much for fear of hurting him or tugging on one of the many tubes connected to him. I couldn't work out why he was here in this state; things like this just don't happen to us, they shouldn't happen to us. But it did, this is the reality – and this reality is not cool.

At the time James was taken away by police and Department of Conservation officials, the next phase of my rescue had already been underway for some time. The next account gives a gripping insight into the actions and thoughts that went through Mark Wood's head as he was unexpectedly informed of Mt Ruapehu's eruption:

> The pizza had just arrived and it smelt great. I grabbed a piece and took a bite just as Andy Hoyle, a member of Ruapehu Alpine Rescue Organisation, beckoned me to come with him.
>
> The look on his face was serious, but when he said, 'the mountain has erupted, Dome Shelter has collapsed and there is a guy pinned in there!' I burst out laughing. He must have been joking.
>
> 'Whatever!' I said and started to make my way back to the pizza.
>
> But Andy grabbed me by the arm and said, 'I'm not kidding.'
>
> I have worked in Ski Patrol and Alpine Rescue on the

WORDS FROM OTHERS: THE COLD HARD FACTS

mountains of the central plateau for twenty-five years and this was by far the most bizarre, unbelievable call I had ever heard.

It was about 9.30 p.m. and we were at a Ski Patrol function at National Park. Andy assembled a team of three: himself, Callum Learmouth and me. We dashed home to grab our gear and headed up the mountain.

I have been through a number of eruptions on Ruapehu over the years so in one sense it was nothing new, but this time there was almost certainly an injured person who was in a bad situation and 'time critical' – we needed to get there as soon as possible.

We regrouped at our Ski Patrol base facility and met with the incident controller. Although it may seem that rescue teams go in to situations 'guns blazing' at great personal risk, this is far from the truth. Once a situation is reported, a well-organised and rehearsed system comes into play. This is known as CIMS – co-ordinated incident management system. All of the emergency services are familiar with the system and comfortably slot into assigned roles. The incident controller is the person running the situation. We were to be the rescue team and were briefed accordingly.

One of our key considerations was whether it was safe for us to go up the mountain at all. We discussed this at length, got information from scientists monitoring the volcano and established points at which we would stop and reconsider what we were doing based on any new information we received.

All indications pointed to the eruption being a 'blue sky' event. This is a one-off event that comes 'out of the blue' and is unlikely to recur. It was a clear night so we decided to go for it.

Andy was appointed as the team leader and I was

assigned to provide patient care. We discussed what gear we would need and double-checked each other's equipment. Two more rescuers were assigned to our team: Nicky Hughes, affectionately known as Shorty, and Phil Smith from the Department of Conservation.

Unfortunately, helicopters weren't prepared to fly there for a number of really valid reasons. Firstly, it was night; it has to be an extremely clear night with settled weather to fly around mountains in the dark! Secondly, the chance of an ash eruption obscuring vision did not justify the risk of flying up there.

So we climbed onto the back of two snow-grooming machines referred to as snowcats. Murray McErlich was driving the lead snowcat. Murray is very experienced at driving these machines and had driven to the Dome Shelter on numerous occasions in the past. This was a huge advantage to us. We also had GPS co-ordinates to get there, but didn't need them thanks to the good visibility and Murray's familiarity with the route up to the shelter.

We headed up the mountain, stopping to get crowbars and shovels from the ski area. When we got to a point about one kilometre from the crater we climbed out of the cats and had a team meeting about whether to proceed or not. It was a beautiful clear night and we could see the lights of National Park Township and Taupo from our vantage point. The air was clear and still but bitterly cold.

One of the volcanic hazards is 'bombs'. These are rock projectiles that are flung out of the crater during an eruption. They rarely go further than one or two kilometres but we drove past a few pretty big bomb craters on the way up. The closer we got to the crater, the greater the risk to all of us if the volcano were to erupt again.

We were happy to go there once we had spoken by telephone to the scientists and the incident controller. We all agreed that minimising our time up there would be the best policy so we headed up at full throttle.

We could clearly see the lahar path as we drove. As we got higher we eventually had to drive right onto the lahar path to get up onto Dome Ridge.

We crested the ridge, driving over a black surface made up of mud, ash and small rocks that had recently been hurled from the volcano. This was a very eerie moment for all of us. It hammered home the gravity of what we were doing. It was like driving on a moonscape and felt very remote and isolated. The outside temperature measured -6°C.

We wasted no time getting to the Dome Shelter, which had taken a hammering but was still intact. I jumped out of the cat and headed for the door with great trepidation.

There was a lot of mud and rocks around and a layer of black ash mixed into the snow covering the building, but the door opened inwards and was quite easy to open.

I pushed myself through the opening and my headlamp cast a dim light into the building. It was full of debris and mud and didn't look good. William came into view. The space he was in was about three metres by one and a half metres. He was sitting up, leaning against the wall with his leg buried to the knee. It wasn't as though his leg was under one rock. The mud, rocks and water that were ejected from the crater had filled the hut by about half a metre and William's leg was encased in this material. Due to the cold temperature the material had frozen solid and set like concrete.

As soon as my light fell on him, William collapsed onto his side. There is a bit of a phenomenon of people in need of rescue managing to hold themselves together against all odds but when the rescue team arrive they relax and inadvertently succumb to the elements and perish. I feared the worst for William.

I squeezed my way up to his head and carefully checked

his vital signs. At this point he made a few mumbling noises but had no detectable pulse at all. I did a quick check of his body, looking for any major injuries, and found that the leg that was not trapped was significantly injured and with obvious deformity.

By this time Callum had squeezed into the small space and was digging around William's trapped leg, stopping to use the crowbar on rocks that he encountered. He did this while I did what I could for William, which wasn't much really. I got some oxygen in him and held his airway open as best I could in the confined space.

Eventually, Callum got to a point where we could extract William's leg. I took control of the leg while Callum moved a bit more debris and got a hold of the foot.

'Are you ready for this, mate?' I asked Callum before we moved the leg.

We could see right from the start that there were horrific injuries.

'Ready as I'll ever be.'

We pulled the leg out. It was totally shattered. Large chunks of bone fell out of the gaping wound in William's flesh. The leg was massively deformed with the foot dangling at a grotesque angle. The wounds were packed with mud and ash. There was no active bleeding happening at this time but he had obviously lost a fair bit of blood. It was clear to us then that there was no way he would be keeping the leg. We put a splint on the leg to stop it from flopping around.

Will was badly injured. He had been doused with water four hours ago and the temperature was about -8°C at this altitude. He was severely hypothermic.

The ideal treatment for an unconscious hypothermic patient is to handle them extremely gently. Any vigorous movement can cause the patient's heart to go into ventricular fibrillation, causing death. I considered all of this but knew

WORDS FROM OTHERS: THE COLD HARD FACTS

that we pretty much had to just pick him up and chuck him in a stretcher and get him out of there as quickly as possible – not to mention getting ourselves out too!

While all this was going on in the hut, the other guys had readied the stretcher and had dug out a trench so they could slide the stretcher in to us. Once we got it inside we just manhandled William into it. It was pretty disconcerting to me knowing that we may well be killing him by our actions but we had no other real choice.

We got the stretcher out and up onto the snowcat. We tied it in, got everybody on board and hightailed it out of there.

Once we had William in a secure workspace, Callum and I went to work on him. We had lined the stretcher with a down sleeping bag, keeping William as protected as possible. We cut off his wet clothes to make a good examination of him, looking for other injuries that we may have missed.

I continued to assess his condition. The machine was noisy and it was hard to look for signs of life, but by now there were none at all that I could find.

As dramatic as this may sound, I was fairly certain that he would not survive the ride down the mountain. He had no pulse at all. I tried rousing him by pinching him hard. I took his temperature in his ear and it read 25°C. Our normal temperature is 37°C. His flesh was waxy and lifeless. When a person is dead, their pupils become fixed and dilated. This means that the pupils are wide open and when you shine a torch into them they do not react to the light at all. William's pupils were fixed and dilated. This was not good at all.

After about three or four minutes I began to detect rapid shallow breathing from William. We normally breathe at about twelve to twenty breaths per minute, but he was breathing at thirty breaths per minute. They were very shallow, barely detectable breaths.

This made no sense to me at all. When a person is hypothermic all of their vital signs slow down until they eventually stop. This was the only sign of life I found at any time on William, once we got him out of the hut. I later learnt that the rapid breathing was probably caused by acidosis from having his leg trapped for such a long time without blood flow. This in turn caused the bad toxins to develop in the leg. His limb was essentially dying when we released it and some of the toxins would have gone into the rest of his bloodstream.

I tried to open William's mouth to get a plastic airway tube in but his jaw and mouth were too frozen. The inside of his mouth, normally a nice pink colour, was a deep blue colour and really cold to the touch. I couldn't get the airway tube into his mouth.

The only encouraging thing was the breathing. To help with this I used a device called a bag valve mask, which allowed me to put a mask over his face and squeeze a bag connected to high-flow oxygen. With the bag I could actually force 100 per cent oxygen into his lungs.

Callum and I kept talking between ourselves, double-checking what we were thinking, making sure we didn't miss anything. I remember feeling quite frustrated that there was nothing more we could do for William. Our objective was to get him off the mountain safely in the best possible condition. Pretty much all we could do was try and stop him getting any colder and package his injuries.

The cat drivers did a fantastic job of racing us down the mountain. We were head-down working on the back of the machine while they powered down the mountain at full speed. We were only really aware of the sound of the motor revving hard and the snow flying up off the machine's tracks. I have no idea how long it took to get down but must have only been fifteen minutes or so.

I finally heard the revs drop and when I looked up I saw that we had arrived at the base of the ski area, where there was a waiting ambulance.

We got William off the cat and onto the ambulance stretcher. I was still acutely aware of all the trauma that we had put him through getting him from the hut into the ambulance. He still had a long way to go to get to somewhere he could get some real treatment that could save his life.

Once we were in the ambulance, I did a handover to the paramedic. I was glad when he asked if I could stay and give him a hand. While the other ambulance officer drove, we went about working on William. We got intravenous lines into both of his arms and repackaged his leg. We dressed his wounds and splinted his other leg. We wrapped him in foil blankets and put blankets around his head and neck. We also put hot-water bottles around his abdomen.

When we got to Whakapapa Village we stopped and microwaved some fluid to put into William through the intravenous lines in the hope of rewarming him.

We continued driving to National Park, which was as close as the helicopters were prepared to come. Once we got there, we had another discussion to make sure we had done all we could for William and finally handed him over to the paramedics on the helicopter.

It was around 2 a.m. It had taken us four hours from the time of the eruption until we got William out of the hut and a further two hours to get him into a helicopter that could get him to a base hospital where they could provide him with the definitive care that he needed.

Mark Woods loaded me into the ambulance at Iwikau Village at 1.12 a.m. At 1.30 a.m. I arrived at National Park. There I was loaded onto the Taupo Lion Foundation Rescue Helicopter at 1.57 a.m. and we landed at Taumarunui Hospital at 2.12 a.m.

Minutes before I arrived in Taumarunui, the A-Zero Westpac rescue team in the Westpac Waikato Air Ambulance helicopter arrived with pilot Simon, specialist emergency physician John Bonning and advanced paramedic Paula John. Dr John Bonning took charge of my care once I landed in Taumarunui. There he began further procedures to keep me alive. John Bonning's account explains the events that took place:

> I was coming to the end of a busy evening shift at Waikato Hospital's emergency department (ED) on September 25th when I got the phone call at 2215 hours to stand by, as Ruapehu had erupted. I had been near the mountain during the 1995/96 eruptions and had been climbing and skiing on Ruapehu since the 70s, so I knew the power it was capable of.
>
> Earlier in the month I had been staying at the Iwikau Village with my son's school ski team and I wondered if anyone there had been affected.
>
> Often when there is a major trauma the situation can initially be unclear. This time we didn't know what had happened on the mountain – whether it was a major eruption like in the mid-1990s or something less spectacular. I heard that there were casualties and initially we didn't know whether it was one or many, nor did we know what condition they were going to be in. Whenever I get a call about a serious incident and we are expecting to have a seriously ill or injured patient brought into the ED, my adrenaline starts pumping with excitement and anticipation of the challenge ahead. At around 0100 hours the A-Zero retrieval team of Simon the pilot, Paula the advanced paramedic and I took off in the Westpac rescue helicopter for Taumarunui. There

was still a lot of uncertainty as to how the volcano was going to behave for us. The Department of Conservation had told us it was unsafe to land on the volcano itself. Given the wind direction driving a potential volcanic ash cloud north towards Taupo, we elected to land at Taumarunui Hospital, which is on the most direct route between Ruapehu and Waikato Hospital.

I liaised with Graeme Harvey, the chief advanced paramedic in Taupo, and we tried to work out where it was going to be safe to meet and stabilise the injured patient or patients.

At the same time as we left Waikato Hospital, the Turangi ambulance arrived at the Iwikau Shelter to retrieve William and take him down to National Park. The Taupo helicopter with Graeme Harvey aboard arrived at National Park around the same time.

Given that we couldn't take a helicopter onto the mountain, we decided that this was the best and quickest way to transport William to the closest hospital for emergency stabilisation before he could be taken to Waikato Hospital.

While the Westpac helicopter was fully equipped with appropriate instruments for flying at night, our pilot Simon did not have night vision goggles. Our radar showed that there was cloud about us in the air, so, at times, we opened the air vents in the helicopter to make sure it was cloud and not volcanic ash we were flying in. Ash is corrosive to the helicopter turbines and could potentially cause catastrophic engine failure.

We are lucky to have such good pilots for our rescue helicopters, as our lives are in their hands. They alone make the decision as to whether it is safe to fly or not.

At 0130 hours we arrived at Taumarunui Hospital. Many local medical staff had got out of bed to come and help us, including nursing staff, laboratory personnel and radiographers to take X-rays. By now we knew we were about to receive an extremely ill young male, although other details were very sketchy. There was a great sense of anticipation.

At this time the Taupo helicopter met the Turangi ambulance in National Park and they very carefully transferred William onto the helicopter for the next segment of his trip north.

William arrived at Taumarunui Hospital at 0212 hours. I went out to the helicopter when it landed and had a discussion with Graeme Harvey as to his state and the best course of action. By this time William was barely conscious but was occasionally trying desperately to wake up. This struggle was the first sign I saw of his incredible fighting spirit: the spirit that ultimately pulled him through his ordeal.

One of William's main problems was that he was suffering from profound hypothermia. His extremely low body temperature meant that his heart was vulnerable to even small insults such as the knocks and movement caused by transferring from one stretcher to another, or by even his own fight to wake up. We were worried that his heart would begin to fibrillate and stop pumping. Should this occur it would be enormously difficult to restart his heart until his body was warmed. With this degree of hypothermia this procedure can only be done in major hospitals. We all instinctively knew that William was literally seconds from death.

When I first saw William in the back of the Taupo rescue helicopter he was cocooned in warm blankets. All I could see in the darkness was his face, which had some abrasions as a result of his ordeal. I could hear him moaning at times. His body temperature was 27°C. Ironically, whilst the cold temperature is damaging to many body tissues, to a degree it actually protects the brain from damage. We felt that as he warmed even slightly he might become more awake, but he would also be in a position where he could harm himself by struggling. It is dangerous to have a semi-conscious patient thrashing about in the cramped back of a helicopter, let alone one whose body temperature is 27°C. I elected to bring William in to Taumarunui Hospital to stabilise him prior to taking him to Waikato Hospital.

We took extreme care as we transferred William from the helipad outside Taumarunui Hospital into the resuscitation room in the ED. I had numerous thoughts flashing rapidly through my mind: I was struck by just how cold he felt to touch; I knew we were walking on a very high tightrope to get William up to Waikato Hospital alive.

Another bizarre feature in this unusual situation was that there were down feathers everywhere from William's jacket, which had been cut to allow access to his arm so that we could give him intravenous fluids and pain relief. There was also the faint sulphurous smell of volcanic ash.

I had to assess the situation very rapidly and rally the team of willing assistants to do various things in order to stabilise William. In a resuscitation room there can be up to ten or more doctors, nurses and paramedics, all of whom perform vital tasks in the team effort of resuscitating a very sick or injured patient. I was very grateful for all the skilled and willing assistants in Taumarunui Hospital, as well as for Paula, the advanced paramedic. Without the large team of specialists that we have at Waikato Hospital, I knew the buck stopped with me if anything should go wrong in this precarious situation.

After I ascertained that William's airway was clear, that he was breathing spontaneously on oxygen and that he had a pulse (albeit very slow) and a cardiac output, I had a quick look at his legs. Lifting the blankets up I was confronted with a lower leg with an enormous crater in it. The crater was grey with volcanic ash and I picked a few pieces of rock out of the gaping hole. His shin bone was totally shattered and the foot beyond it was pale, battered and bruised – it looked dead. I immediately thought to myself, He'll most certainly lose his leg, now what can I do to ensure he doesn't lose his life as well?

His left leg was also pale and battered with a clearly smashed knee cap and some minor wounds.

We rapidly set about preparing William to be intubated. That means that he would be put into a drug-induced coma, then a tube would be inserted into his trachea or windpipe and he would be put onto a mechanical ventilator.

Everyone in the room had a delegated responsibility – establishing further intravenous access, giving William warm intravenous fluids and oxygen, getting cardiac monitors on, preparing all the drugs and equipment. There was a flurry of activity as we checked with each other that everything was ready.

With everybody primed and ready at William's bedside, we gave the appropriate drugs – a mix of agents that take away pain, sedate and paralyse the patient. With the aid of a special instrument called a laryngoscope, I placed a tube through William's mouth, throat, then vocal cords and into his trachea. Of all the things that we did, this was the most likely to precipitate a cardiac arrest so we were relieved when it all went smoothly.

William was still very unstable. He was cold, and his pulse was very slow at around forty beats per minute. We could not record an accurate blood pressure nor could we ascertain the oxygen level in his blood. It was time to package our patient for a safe trip up to Waikato and definitive care. We removed as much of his wet clothing as possible (complete with feathers!), swathed him in warm blankets, gave warm intravenous fluids and prepared to set off.

After the adrenaline and excitement of the resuscitation room in Taumarunui, the helicopter trip home was comparatively quiet and uneventful. There wasn't much we could do other than handle William very carefully and try to coax his heart to continue pumping. He was now quiet and still in a drug-induced coma. We radioed ahead to Waikato Hospital to mobilise the trauma team of emergency doctors, intensivists, anaesthetists and orthopaedic and general surgeons to meet us in Waikato Hospital ED.

At 0400 hours, Paula and I wheeled William into the resuscitation room at Waikato ED and immediately began to plan the timing of the next steps to save his life and try to save his legs.

I had detailed discussions with all the members of the trauma team. We all agreed that we had relatively little experience with dealing with such profoundly hypothermic trauma victims but we quickly formulated a plan. We needed to ascertain whether William had any internal injuries, as well as dealing with his obvious leg injuries.

At this stage I became aware of Barry and Tracy, William's parents, in the background of the resuscitation room. Because of the long lead time from the eruption to our arrival, they had arrived from Auckland before we had. As soon as I could, I went over to them to put them fully in the picture.

When confronted with raw fear and emotion from anxious family members I find it impossible to stay detached and unemotional myself. This is one of the most difficult parts of our job. Both of William's parents were clearly shaken and anxious for news. I outlined to them what I knew to have happened on the mountain – which wasn't much, as these details were still sketchy – and, more specifically, what we had done for him and what we felt the outlook was. It is very important to be direct and give realistic expectations.

I told them it was good to have come this far, but that William was by no means out of the woods. He was still critically ill and there was still a chance of a bad outcome. I told them he would lose at least one leg, that he might have a brain injury or that he might in fact yet die. These are words no parent ever wants to hear and they were shattered at the news, but they maintained their composure as we outlined how we were going to treat him.

I now formally handed over William's care to the anaesthetists and intensivists who would co-ordinate his care as he was being warmed up to the point where surgery would be safe.

The orthopaedic doctors cleaned his wounds and splinted both legs pending formal fixation in the operating theatre. We ascertained from one of our Swedish anaesthetists, who had experience dealing with profoundly cold patients, that we had to warm William to 32°C before it was safe to embark on the major surgery that his legs clearly required.

At this stage I realised just how tired I was – it was nearly 0600 hours and I had been awake for just under twenty-four hours. With such an extraordinary case to deal with I had had no difficulty staying focused, but with the weight of responsibility safely passed into the hands of the specialists who would care for William I was ready for a rest.

I knew that despite his critical condition, we were now in a good position to treat him with all the skill and facilities a top-level tertiary hospital has. I took a last glance at William, looking peacefully sedated on the ventilator, his heart rate and body temperature slowly improving. I hoped fervently for a good outcome. He was a young man with so much potential – I didn't want his life to be tragically wasted.

A few days later when I went up to see William in intensive care, I was delighted to find that he had been taken off the ventilator and was conscious and able to talk. I knew that it must have taken an enormous will to live and great inner strength for him to pull through. It also clearly helped that he was in such great physical shape prior to the accident. Any lesser mind and body may very well not have pulled through. Seeing him propped up in bed brought tears to my eyes.

I shook his hand and introduced myself.

In the ambulance with Mark Woods, bound for National Park to meet the Taupo Lion Foundation Rescue helicopter, my condition began to deteriorate. My heart rate was sixty beats per minute and my blood pressure was 120/95. My normal resting heart rate is sixty-five beats per minute and my normal blood pressure is 120/80.

I arrived at National Park at 1.30 a.m. After the short flight in the Taupo Lion Foundation Rescue Helicopter, piloted by Dan Harcourt, I arrived at Taumarunui Hospital at 1.57 a.m. My heart rate was ninety-nine beats per minute and my blood pressure had dropped to 94/35. After being stabilised as much as possible I left in the Westpac Waikato Air Ambulance, bound for Waikato Hospital, at 3.25 a.m.

I arrived at 3.56 a.m. in Waikato Hospital's emergency department. My heart rate had dropped further, to forty beats per minute. My blood pressure had also dropped to 65/29.

In the emergency department I received multiple blood transfusions to replace the huge amount of blood that I'd lost.

My severely hypothermic condition and the likely outcomes from being so cold were something the doctors and nurses had very little experience with. My 25°C body temperature was the lowest any doctors from the Waikato Hospital had ever come across (other than for a dead person). New Zealand is a relatively warm country where body temperatures as low as mine are unheard of. There was a chance I had suffered from brain injuries and other unknown related symptoms resulting from my profound hypothermic condition.

Before I was taken to theatre for surgeons to accurately assess my wounds, I needed to have a body temperature of 32°C or above. Otherwise it was feared that the anaesthetics would stop my heart, resulting in death.

When Dr John Bonning had done everything possible to help me, I was handed over to Waikato Hospital's specialist doctors and nurses at 6.15 a.m. My body temperature was officially recorded at 27.7°C after considerable rewarming attempts.

Due to breakthrough bleeding and further considerable blood loss, I was given four units of blood and four units of fresh frozen plasma. All fluids that were administered into my bloodstream were warmed in a microwave first.

In the hands of Waikato Hospital's specialist doctors and nurses I was taken to a room where they warmed my body up with a device described by my parents as a paper thin lilo that lay over me like a blanket. It had warm air pumped through its small holes and onto me. At this stage, my heart rate was forty-five beats per minute. My blood pressure had risen to 77/29. The biggest fear the doctors had was that the smallest bump or knock I received could give me a heart attack. I was handled with ultimate care.

Once my body had reached 32°C I was rushed off to have a CT scan of my brain, spine and abdominal area. Amazingly there were no head, back or abdominal injuries. However, extensive pockets of pressurised air were noted around my heart, possibly due to the volcanic explosion. Immediately after the CT scans I was rushed to theatre for emergency surgery.

My parents and brother were notified of my accident just after Mark Woods and his team reached me in the Dome Shelter. Below their thoughts, feelings and emotions are shared. It was a night they will never forget.

A Night To Remember ... 26 September 2007

Although the world is full of suffering,
it is also full of the overcoming of it.
AUTHOR UNKNOWN

As a parent, I felt secure as I watched the late night news. Breaking news announced that Mt Ruapehu had erupted at approximately 8.20 p.m. I knew William and James would be at the Dome Shelter, on the second day of their exciting planned climbs.

Barry was asleep so I woke him to say Ruapehu had erupted – not spectacular news.

William was extremely careful in planning his climbs and we knew his detailed itinerary.

Andrew came home a little later, and I mentioned the eruption.

'No worries there, Mum,' was Andrew's comment.

For some reason I did not settle into sleep.

At 12.50 a.m. I was startled by a very loud knocking on our front door – a sound I will always remember.

Barry, Andrew and I all leapt out of bed. As we went to answer that insistent knocking, we all felt fear and dread, but that knock just had to be answered.

Four police officers were on our doorstep – now that is a dread that no parent ever wants to feel, as you know they are not about to deliver good news.

The police officer who stepped forward was about to

change our lives – his name was Sam Wood, and he was a childhood friend of William's. He had solemn news to deliver.

'William has been in an accident on Mt Ruapehu earlier this evening and he has sustained serious injuries – William's life is in a status one condition.'

I clearly remember saying to Sam, 'Status one, what is that?'

By this time I was beginning to feel shock. I was cold, standing there in my pyjamas in the middle of our dining room with four police officers. One officer was on the phone trying to get current information on William's whereabouts and condition.

Sam was explaining that when a person has injuries, their injuries are classified from status five, where they require very little medical attention, to status one, where a person is not expected to survive . . .

We were being told that our full-of-life, wired-for-adventure son and brother's body was injured to such an extent that he may not be alive when we see him next. How could that possibly be?

William certainly lived life to the max, and challenged every day. He was always climbing in his own wonderland – I was so sure that he was safe.

The police told us he was at Taumarunui Hospital and would be airlifted to Waikato Hospital as soon as he was stabilised.

Barry, Andrew and I were all in shock, almost unable to believe what we had just been told. Sam told us we should leave for Waikato Hospital immediately. William would be arriving there by helicopter soon.

I could not imagine William arriving at hospital with life-threatening wounds without us there to meet him.

Sam and the other officers left us in a state of disbelief.

WORDS FROM OTHERS: THE COLD HARD FACTS

We made phone calls we thought were important – what is important at this time? One call to my manager at work, one to one of William's close friends, one to our wonderful neighbour who arrived in the middle of the night to be with us.

Andrew made some calls as we all hastily gathered what we thought we would need before we began our two-hour drive to be with William.

We played Sublime, one of William's favourite bands, as we drove. It was a quiet drive, none of us spoke much. We had no idea what to expect when we saw William again.

We arrived at Waikato Hospital emergency department at about 3.40 a.m., to be met by an emergency department nurse. She was expecting us and led us to the rear of the ED to a lonely, quiet room. Once there, she asked us to sit down.

Sit down! That was the last thing we wanted to do. We wanted news of William. Where was he? What was his condition? When would he be arriving?

We were glad that we had arrived before William but seeing the emergency department nurse with tears in her eyes as she spoke to us was frightening.

Barry, Andrew and I watched silently as a stretcher was wheeled towards us. How could that be William on that stretcher? That stretcher, surrounded by life-saving equipment and staff, meant serious injuries to William and devastation to our family. We waited together for our cherished son and brother to complete our family circle.

Our lives had changed uncontrollably. How we were all going to cope was intensely individual.

We entered the resuscitation room, a family of four together, unconditionally united.

Was this William before us?

Yes.

But ohhh! He was asleep, covered in grey ash. There were

burns and small lacerations visible and he was surrounded with intravenous tubes.

He was so cold to touch – so still – in an induced coma, with a body temperature of 27°C.

This was our William!

Experts dressed in blue scrubs acknowledged our presence and then began their life-preserving work.

We reluctantly realised there was tension in the resus room. William had severe life-threatening injuries.

Staff gave us access to William. We could talk to him and we prayed that he could hear us. The three of us held his hands and touched his body, hoping our body temperatures might help to warm him – hoping the power of spirit and human touch would make everything all right!

At times the doctors worked around us. We could now see all of William's injuries – those legs that hours before had been climbing mountains and walking through life lay before us with unimaginable injuries. His bones were protruding, there was no skin, his muscles were crushed and his foot was lifeless – this really was our William.

We tried to remain calm and composed. Silent tears were shed as we listened, watched and loved.

We were given access to a telephone and told to call relatives and friends. 'William is critically ill and is by no means out of the woods, he will certainly lose one leg, he may have a brain injury and he may yet die'... This was the news we had to convey to our loved ones.

I don't know how Barry, Andrew and I took all of this in, let alone had the strength to relay and describe what was unfolding before us...

It was still early in the morning, around 5 a.m., as we called family, trying to share these moments with them. Standing beside a microwave that was used to warm the fluids being administered to William, we tried to let family know our news before any of them heard news bulletins or saw a newspaper. While making the phone calls, we had to rush to William's bedside as his condition worsened.

How do you describe your world crumbling around you while your loved son and brother silently fights for his life?

We shall forever be grateful that we were given so much access to William as he lay so lifeless in the resus room.

Medical decisions were made as to how quickly to warm William's body. Would his left leg be saved? Would his heart be able to cope with all that was happening?

At this time the love within our family could not have been stronger as we talked to devastated grandparents, brothers and sisters who would soon be at our sides.

Barry, Andrew and I unconditionally undertook the beginning of a journey. We had no idea where it would take us, we just needed to be by William's side as he fought for his life, to be together as we all suffered privately.

William was now in the greatest of medical care at Waikato Hospital and we had to believe that we would always be a family of four.

The terrifying time that my close family experienced that night was unwillingly shared later by my extended family and friends. A close friend of mine writes here how he found out about my accident, and of times with me in hospital. Having known me for nearly ten years, Matthew Harrison (a.k.a. Matt, Harry, Harold, H, Apple Head) writes with humour, wit and nothing but the truth!

Being a mildly popular young man, I wasn't too surprised to have two text messages greet me as I awoke from my disjointed slumber on the morning of 26 September 2007. However, what did surprise and slightly disappoint me was that they were both from my old man. Great, I sarcastically thought to myself, wondering what he might want to pester me about.

Now, I'm generally not a huge fan of getting up at 6.30 on a good day (unlike the writer of this book), but to have two text messages from my dad isn't usually an overly positive sign. I have come to learn that it generally means that I'm either late for work and he's disgruntled or I'm really late for work and he's left without me. On the morning of 26 September it was neither of those two things. It was instead far more ominous and simply read, 'Call me asap'.

Human nature dictates situations like these and automatically I asked myself who had died. Nobody sends vague messages, wanting to talk to you, without it being something serious. Intermittent hot flushes washed across me from my forehead to my feet. Having no credit on my phone I sent a text back to ask Dad to ring me.

In a low voice he said, 'Hi Matt. William has...' At this point I knew immediately Pike was hurt. Dad wouldn't call Pike 'William' unless he's been naughty or something's not right. I absorbed what he had to say; obviously it wasn't great news. Dad had heard the news at 2 a.m. that morning when he got a call from Barry and Tracy as they sped down to Hamilton.

He held off telling me until the morning. I guess there was nothing I could have done but worry, but that morning I was annoyed that he hadn't told me earlier. I just wanted to teleport straight to Waikato Hospital. I just wanted more information. I paced around wondering what to do. Do I get in my car and go? Do I wait to hear from the Pikes? I fired off text messages to Andy Pike and started letting our close friends know.

As disbelief and uncertainty swirled around, I rushed to the TV and newspaper, both of which had vague coverage.

It was around 8 a.m. or 9 a.m. that morning when I first saw Bill; well it wasn't really all of him, just his pale blue feet poking out from underneath a mass of rescuers and reflective warming blankets. When you see this kind of thing on the news your mind races. Your body goes into a nervous autopilot state. Your wander aimlessly. You find yourself standing somewhere you don't remember walking to. My mind was in Hamilton . . . unfortunately my body was stuck in Auckland.

Seconds seem like minutes and the optimistic and pessimistic parts of your brain start squaring off against each other — you say to yourself, 'Everything will be fine, it's Pike we're talking about here. The kid is one of the most cautious and well-organised people I have ever met.' Unfortunately it is the negative part that is hardest to handle. You know you shouldn't think negatively but it's hard not to remind yourself that eruptions have a fairly decent reputation for killing people.

Towards mid-morning I received a call from Andrew Pike telling me that one of Bill's legs was to be amputated, with the real possibility that they may need to take both. With so many questions and very few answers I just stood there unsure of what to do or who to talk to. I was completely idle and transfixed as I watched and listened to every news bulletin possible.

By this time word had spread and all of our friends were shattered by the news. After speaking to Andrew, we were told not to rush down as the family needed to spend some time evaluating the situation uninterrupted. This failed to stop us. We didn't care whether we got to see him or not, we just wanted to be as close as possible. The car was packed with an array of scattered belongings and four very sombre occupants.

The journey down was very therapeutic. Being around

people who are feeling just the way you are makes things a lot easier. We talked openly, offering our personal interpretations about what we had heard, what we had seen, who we had spoken to and how bad we thought the situation was. The motorway was quiet and we ended up passing a group of our friends travelling down in another car. We stopped, chatted and once again exchanged information. A lot of the things said were repetitive and speculative but it's the reassurance of being together that is most valuable.

We arrived at the hospital and were promptly surrounded by reporters scrounging for information. We abruptly said we knew very little and gathered ourselves to go in. After a relatively vocal trip down, it quickly became very quiet as each of us began to wonder what we were about to see and hear. I was apprehensive and unwittingly tense. After wandering through the sterile halls of Waikato Hospital – which were to become a frequent weekend destination for us in the following weeks – we arrived at the waiting room to be greeted by Barry and Tracy. It was at this point that we realised how serious it was. Seeing your best friend's mum and dad in tears is pretty awful. Greetings and hugs were exchanged in a blur. Barry and Tracy then sat us down to explain the situation.

It was bad. Bill was as close to dead as the doctors at Waikato had ever seen and the next few hours were going to be an agonising waiting game. Despite Bill's poor condition, the doctors had stabilised him enough to allow brief visits.

Seeing him for the first time was surreal. Tubes from loud beeping machines tangled their way around his body and bed into almost every orifice. Doctors and nurses busily took notes, checked the life-preserving machines and spoke in a foreign language full of medical jargon. We were told to stand either side of the bed and hold one of his hands – they were small, cold and smelt like sulphur. At this point he had a hospital blanket covering his lower half. Curiosity insisted that you looked down to where his lower right leg should be but the blanket simply dropped off at his knee.

We chatted away, trying to think of things to say that wouldn't require his response. Every so often his eyes would open and his hands clench or he'd utilise his dive signals and give us the 'A-O-K' or 'thumbs-down' to let us know what he was thinking. But to be honest, he wasn't thinking at all. It wasn't until weeks later that we found out that he didn't remember the first two weeks at all and concluded that morphine was doing most of the talking. I guess the best way to describe his state when I saw him for the first time was like a fish out of water – wide eyed, clammy and surging every so often with erratic movements (and minus a fin of course).

Too worried to go home, the strong contingent of Bill's friends spent the night in a motel, glued to the TV, playing cards and having a few beers. We even managed a few laughs, at Bill's expense of course. Even though we weren't down there for a particularly joyous occasion, we knew it's what Bill would have wanted and it really helped talking about it with the odd infusion of laughter.

The following two months involved a lot of trips down to Hamilton. In the whole two or so months I don't think he had a single day when no one visited. One night I promised to stay over to relieve Tracy of the honourable duty of emptying and replacing his bedpan. Minor spillages on the way to the sluice room meant that I didn't get asked to do that job again in a hurry. It was an interesting night for me. Although this was towards the end of Bill's stay in Waikato it was the first time I really had a decent chance to talk to him about that night. Every other time there were dressing changes, pills to be swallowed, plastic surgeon appointments, toilet appointments (the one thing you get used to with Bill pretty quickly is that he has a bladder the size of an acorn) and numerous other important but frustrating interruptions. It was on that night that he pragmatically told me that he had thought he was going to die, firstly from drowning as the slurry of ash and melted ice rose quickly above his chest, and secondly from hypothermia. His voice never broke, it simply radiated unwavering fortitude. We chatted for a while until he asked if I wanted to see photos of his leg before it was amputated. Unaware that there were photos, I was taken aback but extremely curious. I flicked through, casually thinking to myself that they weren't too bad, only X-rays and a few slides with medical info. Without warning I was greeted by a picture showing the insides of his right calf, clearly showing the tendons, muscles, fat and blood. It gave me a real appreciation of the need to amputate. Without going into too much detail, his ankle was completely rotated and his foot was facing the wrong way. He had several gashes up and down the leg and they were filled with ash and debris, despite a thorough cleaning. Bones, snapped in half, protruded from the open wounds. His lower right leg was ruined; keeping it was not an option. The graphic photos showed the necessity of the life-changing surgery.

Over the recovery period many things were reported by the various forms of media, who were at times entirely accurate, but more often than not their information was skewed. It really made me realise that when you read things in the paper or hear them on the news, a certain amount of scepticism is required. Not everything you hear from the media is true.

On the other hand, there was some amazing support from the likes of John Campbell, who, despite not being someone I personally enjoy watching, I have a large amount of respect for after dealing with his professional crew. The thing with Pike is that over the years he has met and made a lasting impression on many people ... people from next door, people from down the road, people from overseas (and, yes, even people from Australia). The problem with this was that there were so many people wanting and needing to know how he was going that it made it difficult for Barry, Tracy and Andrew to keep on top of the 200 odd text messages a day and heaps of phone calls. The web provided the perfect solution, and with help of Daniel Charles Jehovah Grant (a.k.a. Orange Man), the 'Pikeinfo' email was born. It simply outlined what had happened recently, what was expected to happen and any other little bits of information we picked up on that were of interest. It was a good way to keep everyone up to date, especially those scattered across the globe.

As I write this little passage for Bill, I sit here glad to have my friend back to normal. A lot of you will probably stop and say, 'He isn't normal; he survived an eruption and is now disabled.' In a way you're a lot like his amputated leg ... half right, half wrong. He has survived an eruption, severe hypothermia and weeks of surgery and ongoing rehabilitation. He is definitely not normal. Normal people do not survive such events. Normal people pass away and give up. He is a survivor and is by no means normal.

But let me assure you, he is definitely not disabled, far from it in fact. The doctors didn't amputate his sense of humour, his love for the outdoors, or his family and friends. Sure, he has to wait until his leg is healed well enough to have a prosthetic fitted, but I can promise you that this won't be the last time you hear of William Walter (Walter ahahahahaha) Pike.

Bill isn't disabled, he's just Bill again.

CHAPTER NINE

CHASING DREAMS

Whatever you vividly imagine, ardently desire and enthusiastically act upon must inevitably come to pass.
ADVENTURE PHILOSOPHY TEAM

I worked full-time at the Dive Centre from December 2002 until I resigned in December 2003. I was happy with the work I was doing but became frustrated with the long hours and six-day week I was working. I knew for certain that I couldn't work like this for the rest of my life. I wanted time to go diving and the opportunity to spend my weekends with family and friends.

My friend's brother, Alex Broome, sat me down one evening after water polo training and suggested I think about being a primary school teacher. He told me that I had the qualities to be a good teacher and that I should consider it as a career option. I appreciated his suggestion and thought about it for a few weeks. I could picture myself as a teacher, relating well with kids, passing on my skills, knowledge and life skills and enjoying the long holidays!

Alex called me a few weeks later and told me that the teachers' college he was attending was having an open day. Luckily it fell on my day off, so I went along, not knowing what to expect.

I briefly met Alex as he rushed off to a class and then I was left to have a wander around. I talked to some lecturers and watched a presentation promoting teaching and the programmes offered by the college. At that stage it was known as the Auckland College of Education: It's now called Auckland University, Faculty of Education.

I took home some pamphlets and information booklets. Over a few nights I read them all carefully and seriously considered becoming a teacher. I took more time to think about what was a big decision to make.

I chatted to my parents, my uncle Jason, who loves his job as a teacher, and a few other teachers I knew. Eventually I made the decision to enrol for teachers' college.

I really liked the thought of helping children and shaping them into New Zealand's future citizens. I felt teaching was a *real* job with an objective other than making as much money as possible. Most companies and businesses are driven by the overall objective of making money. I liked the fact that teaching was not driven entirely by money, instead the objective was to give children the knowledge and skills to participate effectively in society. I believed I could make a difference in some children's lives – no amount of money is worth that.

Applying for teachers' college was a lengthy and detailed process, and it took months before an answer arrived. Late one Saturday afternoon I arrived home from work hot and bothered to find an envelope on my bed from teachers' college. The letter acknowledged my application and accepted it – with one condition. Because my grades from sixth and seventh form were below average, I had to pass the first year or else I would be kicked out of college.

I was so happy, I took the letter out and showed it to a couple of my friends, then threw a big party!

Within the first semester I knew teaching was for me. I did my first two-week teaching placement at Murrays Bay

Intermediate School and was hooked. In my first year I worked damned hard and passed all my assignments, and did so comfortably.

My next teaching placement at Sunnybrae Normal Primary School confirmed my love for teaching and I've never thought of doing another job since.

At university I found out that you can't get much better than the uni student lifestyle. My timetable was cruisy, with classes starting about 9 a.m. or 10 a.m. and finishing by 2 p.m. or 3 p.m. If I didn't want to go to a class, I'd make sure a friend was taking notes for me – though it was in my best interest to attend class, apart from the odd day that was perfect for diving!

Teaching largely is a female-dominated profession, which meant that in my class of thirty-five students, I was one of only five guys. That had its positive and negative points!

Summer holidays went from the end of October to the beginning of March, with a month long mid-semester break. School holidays suited my lifestyle perfectly, allowing me to make extended trips in the outdoors.

I was still playing water polo for the North Sport Water Polo Club in 2004, my first year of university. In that year I started going on my own tramps and outdoor adventures, slowly developing an unbreakable addiction to the outdoors.

I started with small day walks in the local Waitakere Ranges and built up to weekends away in different wilderness areas, then eventually planning and going on week-long expeditions into the remote wilderness of New Zealand.

In the years I had been playing club water polo, I had been in every team that had won the national championship tournament for every possible age group – twice. I started to lose motivation and interest in water polo, as I felt short of a decent challenge. In 2005 I made a life-changing decision to stop playing water polo competitively, to allow me the time to pursue my new challenge and passion – the great outdoors. There simply wasn't the time to do both, and by focusing on one I knew I could achieve my goal of doing as many tramping trips as possible and becoming skilled, experienced and proficient in the bush and outdoors.

It was a huge change, as I was no longer seeing my best mates every day at training and that took months to get used to. Fortunately I had made such strong friendships through water polo, I never stopped seeing my water polo mates and often watch their games.

After finishing water polo I was determined to maintain my physical fitness to a very high level. When in the outdoors, I didn't want to be unfit, hurting, breathless and feeling miserable from the excessive exercise. I wanted to be full of energy, super-fit and strong so that going into the outdoors wouldn't be a chore or a continual physical test. I began to train harder than ever before, with my motivation being an increased enjoyment of the outdoors and maintaining a high level of health and wellbeing – I'm a bit of a health freak!

Each time I went for a bush walk I'd fill my pack with phone books and milk bottles full of water to simulate the weight of the food and equipment needed for a week-long tramp.

Tramping four or five times a week for up to five or six hours wasn't possible, so I bought a road bike. The physical endurance needed for cycling over long periods of time is similar to bush walking, so a road bike was perfect.

When I bought my road bike I started riding for one to two hours a session and slowly built up to three to five hours a session. A typical week of training would consist of a Monday off, a two-hour fast ride on Tuesday, a two-hour easy ride on Wednesday as well as a short run, a three- to four-hour ride on Thursday and something different like a swim or a run on Friday. On Saturday I would do a two- to three-hour ride, with a big bunch ride on Sunday for four or five hours. If I had the time to head out for a bush walk instead of a ride, I'd always prefer to do that. I never went to the gym – I found pumping weights boring and I didn't need the extra weight of bulky muscles. I really enjoyed cycling; it gave me a buzz, I was outside in the fresh air and it was excellent for my health and fitness.

Doing so much exercise meant that I needed to eat the right food. I've always been super-fussy about what goes into my body. I ate a lot of carbohydrates (bread, pasta, rice) for long-lasting energy, as much protein as possible (fish, meat, nuts) and I limited high-fat processed foods. I snacked on energy bars, nuts, fresh fruit and vegetables, as I strongly believe that you are what you eat. By eating healthy food, I knew my body could perform to a high level for long periods of time. Soft drink, pies, lollies and processed junk food are unhealthy and definitely not for me. Junk food doesn't do your body any good and there's no way it can provide the required nutrients for day-to-day living and exercise.

I wanted my body to be in top shape for scuba diving. I wanted to be as efficient as possible with my consumption of air so I could stay under the water for longer. That meant no smoking, as it would seriously affect my lungs for all physical activity and increase my air consumption when diving. Smoking is one of the most disgusting habits I can think of.

I'm puzzled by why people choose to smoke. Every cigarette is doing them irreparable damage. It also damages other people around them and it looks absolutely revolting. I have never once smoked a cigarette or smokable drug of any sort. Not many people believe me when I say that but my close friends know it's true. I never gave in to peer pressure and stuck with what I believed, and I'm proud of that.

I was continually motivated to keep fit and monitor the food I ate and what went into my body. Just like a car, if I kept my body well oiled and fuelled with high-quality food, it would go for a million miles.

In 2005 I planned a tramping trip to Mt Taranaki with a girlfriend. It was one of the first trips that I had researched and planned all by myself. I felt an amazing sense of satisfaction once I had completed the tramp, knowing that I had planned the entire trip. The tramp involved a five-day walk around Mt Taranaki. Most of the tramp was below the bush line, except for one day when we briefly ventured above the bush line into the alpine area. I learnt some very valuable lessons from this tramp. It boosted my confidence in the bush and it sparked my interest in mountaineering.

The first lesson I learnt on that trip is one that I'm still very embarrassed about today. We did the tramp in April, which is in mid-autumn, and I was dead keen to summit Mt Taranaki (2518 metres). I knew there was a high chance there'd be ice on the summit and that I'd need to use crampons.

I rang the Egmont National Park Department of Conservation to get any track updates and to ask for their recommendations. The woman I talked to at DOC recommended that I take crampons in case there was ice near the summit.

It never occurred to me that I would need an ice axe as well. An ice axe is more important than crampons. It can stop you falling if you slip. You can use it to cut steps in ice if you don't have crampons and it is an essential item for travelling on snow – let alone for climbing a moderately dangerous mountain. Thankfully on the only day that we had a chance to summit Mt Taranaki, the weather deteriorated and we decided not to attempt the climb. That bit of bad weather prevented one or both of us from either killing ourselves or ending up seriously injured.

I still find it hard to believe that I knew so little about

using an ice axe and crampons, yet I had been allowed to hire only crampons to reach the summit of the mountain, without any questions asked.

Through that first lesson I can see how easily inexperienced people – in any sport – can get themselves into trouble. Once I realised how incompetent I was, the importance of getting professional tuition to use specialist equipment I was unfamiliar with became really obvious.

I also learnt a couple of other lessons that day: never shortcut any gear requirements and never underestimate the weather. We were both underequipped for travelling above the bush line once the weather deteriorated. We shouldn't have kept going after the wind began to rise, the temperature dropped so rapidly that puddles had a thin layer of ice on them, and the visibility dropped to twenty or thirty metres. Our hands were numbed by the wind and low temperatures. The powerful freezing wind and rain made our eyes sting and water. A good pair of gloves and snow goggles would have made all the difference and we'd have had a much safer and more enjoyable trip.

Although it wasn't snowing, we walked through a lot of snow and over frozen puddles. My girlfriend didn't have gaiters on her boots to stop the snow getting in. More than once she told me that snow was getting into her boots and she couldn't feel her toes. She was terrified of frostbite. She was scared and angry at me for insisting we take the higher route in poor weather when we could have taken the lower and easier route through the bush. I thought the bush route would be boring and the higher route would be more exciting.

As we were getting blown around in gale-force wind and driving rain, I smiled at her and assured her we'd be OK. I didn't want to let on that I was worried about getting lost or becoming hypothermic in the cold conditions too.

While my girlfriend was having a harrowing experience I was secretly having the time of my life. I was loving this new alpine experience and the challenge of poor weather. I remember thinking, Man... this is so awesome and beautiful. As soon as I get home, I'm going to join an alpine club, and get into some mountaineering.

A few weeks later, still on a high from my Mt Taranaki experience, I went to a barbeque with my girlfriend at her friend's place. I was enjoying a juicy steak when this guy walked in the door wearing a climbing jacket and a pair of distinctive outdoor shoes. I immediately thought, This guy looks like a keen outdoors man.

I introduced myself and he told me his name, Cameron Walker, and we got talking. I recognised him from water polo – he played for a different high school. He casually mentioned that he had just been on his first mountaineering trip. For the rest of the afternoon I didn't talk to anyone else. We talked for hours, sharing stories about tramping and the little mountaineering he had done. At the end of the day we organised a five-day mountaineering trip to the Tongariro National Park. I didn't sleep that night, I was so excited.

A week later I got a call from Cameron to see if I was still interested in doing the trip. It was a silly question really! I was over-excited and still losing sleep thinking about what mountaineering would be like. I told Cameron I didn't have any mountaineering equipment, so I gratefully took up his offer to lend me his dad's helmet, ice axe and crampons.

The following week we began the five-day trip, both curious to see if we would enjoy each other's company. On the second day of the trip we had walked high enough to encounter the snow, ice and rocks. Cameron introduced me to the basics of mountaineering and I climbed my first mountain – Mt Tongariro (1967 metres).

Climbing with an ice axe came naturally to me, and

I felt comfortable and safe as we climbed higher and the distance to fall became greater. On top of Mt Tongariro I was speechless at the beauty of the new environment. It was like nothing I had ever seen before and I instantly became addicted to mountaineering.

That afternoon we pitched Cameron's tent in the south crater, close to the saddle between Mt Ngauruhoe and Mt Tongariro. We had a suspicion that bad weather was on its way and built a huge snow wall around the tent with Cameron's shovel. It was pretty flash and we were impressed with our first-time efforts.

The next morning we woke up to a full-scale blizzard. We awkwardly geared up in the very cramped tent and went outside to assess the wild weather. We could see no more than thirty metres in front of us and found it difficult to walk upright in the gale-force winds. We decided it was unsafe to go anywhere and spent the next two days in our cramped, cold and smelly tent.

Unfortunately, I found out that my bowels – just like yours – don't stop working in a blizzard. After one and a half days in the tent, my bowels were about to let loose. I geared up for the blizzard in boots, a beanie, snow goggles, jacket, overpants, gloves and warm underlayers. I reluctantly left the tent, picking up toilet paper and my shovel on the way.

As soon as I got outside, my face was sandblasted by the wind, which was carrying millions of snow crystals. The wind and driving snow felt like a never-ending sand storm stinging my face; I'll never forget it. I stopped next to an outcrop of ice-coated rocks, about head high, but not providing any shelter from the wicked wind. I was frightened at the thought of pulling my pants down and exposing my goods to the stinging ice storm but I had no choice. I dug a small, deep hole, a bit like a long drop. I squatted down, with the toilet paper in my hand thrashing in the gale like a cut snake.

The worst thing I thought could happen was the contents of my bowels getting accidentally caught amongst my underwear, thermals, shorts and overpants – imagine dealing with that revolting mess with no washing machine or spare clothes to escape the smell. However, I guess by the time I got back to the tent it would be frozen like dry mud and I could have picked and flicked it out! But I was lucky, as the brown torpedoes fell gracefully into the snow, like an Olympic pool diver, without a splash. Thankfully they didn't land in my pants!

My hands were freezing and my underwear, thermals and overpants were full of snow. Anyone watching would have been in fits of laughter.

When I got back to the tent and got undressed from all my clothing, I got back into my warm, comfortable sleeping bag. Cameron and I had a good laugh about my toileting experience. To my delight, I got the last laugh, as Cameron needed to go to the toilet after me!

For the rest of the time we had a blast and were actually excited to be stuck in a blizzard. We told each other story after story and got to know each other very well. Luckily we enjoyed each other's company, and we even began to plan our next mountain trip and our next tramping trip. From then on Cameron became my number one climbing partner and we went on to do countless climbing trips and other outdoor adventures.

After Cameron and I returned from our mind-blowing adventure, we put together a slide show with the photos from our trip and added some quotes at the end. We were so inspired and motivated by our adventure that we felt the need to share it with other people so they could see some of what we experienced. I showed it to a lot of my friends and family, but photos can never offer the exact experience that the photographer had when they were taking them. A lot of people I showed enjoyed looking at the photos but couldn't understand why we went to such an effort to get ourselves into such a harsh and uncomfortable environment and then actually enjoyed it. I tried my best to explain why I had enjoyed the trip but most people thought I was a bit crazy to want to go through so much discomfort to be in the mountains.

One quote at the end of the slide show read:

In the landscape of each and every human imagination lies one special place. Our inner compass keeps pointing us towards this spot, which is magnetic, mysterious, exotic, and alluring but, alas, always fringed by a frontier of our fears. Still, it is to this specific place that we are compelled to travel in order to know ourselves and, in so doing, call our lives complete.
ALVAH SIMON, *NORTH TO THE NIGHT*

Cameron and I liked this quote because it reminded us of our trip, but back then I *couldn't* fully relate to it, mainly because I was a very inexperienced mountaineer. It wasn't until two years and many mountaineering trips later that I reread this quote and *could* fully relate to it.

I wouldn't call myself an experienced mountaineer now, rather an experienced bush walker and intermediately skilled mountaineer. This quote means a lot to me now and perfectly describes my attraction to mountaineering. It has helped me understand why I love this activity that is misunderstood by so many people.

The quote comes from Alvah Simon's fascinating book, *North to the Night*. Alvah and his wife Diana sail as far north as possible, to the Arctic Circle, in the summer. When they can sail no further because of ice, he anchors his boat with the intention of wintering over. When winter comes around in the Arctic Circle a large percentage of the Arctic Ocean freezes solid.

Alvah intentionally allows his boat to be frozen solid amongst the Arctic Ocean. When Diana's father gets sick, she is flown out on a rescue helicopter to be with him. On his own for six months, Alvah endures temperatures of below -20°C, polar bear threats and hypothermia, as well as other mental and physical challenges.

Alvah writes about his mysterious inner desire to experience the harsh and dangerous Arctic environment in a simple but beautiful setting. This quote is the best thing I've read in an attempt to describe the desire to be in such an undesirable place.

My imagination is dominated by the mountains. I have a mad obsession with mountaineering. When I wake up in the morning I'm thinking about mountaineering. On the way to work I'll be thinking about a mountaineering trip that I have done or would like to do. At lunchtime, when eating my cheese, Marmite and salami sandwiches, I'm reminded of sitting in the snow, carving salami and cheese with my filthy unwashed pocket knife and slapping it on to a Marmite cracker. When I'm on the toilet I'll be reading one of forty climbing magazines that live on the toilet floor. When eating dinner I'll be telling a story about a mountaineering trip or discussing potential trips. Once I get to bed I'll be reading a book about mountaineering. It's safe to say that on any given day I will have thought about mountaineering at least a hundred times.

Alvah Simon writes about an 'inner compass' being magnetic, mysterious, exotic, alluring and fringed with fear. Somewhere in my brain I have developed an inner compass that magnetically draws me to all that is associated with mountaineering. Everything about mountaineering is alluring to me and captivates me in so many ways, acting as my inner compass. A few things spring to mind when I think about *what* it actually is about mountaineering that I'm attracted to. However, I find it extremely difficult to say *why* I'm attracted to these things.

The first thing that springs to mind is the squeak created by my boots when walking on soft snow and the distinctive crunching noise created as my crampons puncture or scratch the ice's surface as I'm walking or climbing.

I'm amazed by the awe-inspiring beauty of Mother Nature's simple elements: ice, snow and rock, which can be transformed into complex works of art. Just being in a mountain environment makes me feel privileged to experience what few people will ever see in their entire life. It makes me appreciate how lucky I am to have the opportunity to do these things. The blood, sweat and tears mixed with the extraordinary physical and mental strength that's needed to perform safely and effectively in a mountain environment give me an unmatched sense of self-satisfaction, pleasure and pride.

I love gear, talking about gear, using gear and shopping for gear. I'm a gear freak – I love high-tech toys for boys (and girls of course!) I like the lightest, toughest and best-quality gear, so long as it's going to do the job, keep me safe, keep me alive and perform in some of the worst conditions on planet earth. Climbing is a gear-intensive sport and I get my thrills using a wide range of cool gear. Being a gear freak does have one negative point – my bank balance is continually taking a hammering, as good gear does not come cheap!

A *full understanding* of respect, trust, true friendship, confidence, good communication skills, loads of life skills and your body's limits can be discovered through mountaineering.

As a general rule, I like to plan well, be prepared, be careful and to take time to think through ideas and options. I don't like to put myself into any situation of great danger. I'm not saying that mountaineering is the be-all and end-all, because I enjoy so many other sports too.

It is pretty weird that mountaineering is my favourite sport considering the constantND dangers it presents: avalanches, rock and ice falls, hypothermia, getting lost, falling from a great height, snow blindness, sunburn, dehydration, frost bite and now, it seems, volcanic eruptions!

Along with the many dangers come the discomforts of being in a mountain environment. You don't have the luxuries of home – no flush toilet, no kettle or microwave, no heater to keep you warm and no house to walk into when the weather turns nasty. Everything in the mountains is fifty times more difficult than at home. You get to wear the same clothes for seven days without deodorant or a shower. You sleep on one-centimetre-thick foam mattresses and you eat high-energy food with low taste day after day.

The physical strength and endurance required to walk and climb in cold conditions with a heavy pack, day after day, requires an extremely high standard of fitness and a high pain threshold. When you're on a steep climb and your calf muscles are jittering like a sewing machine needle, there's often no other option but to keep going. You require an even mix of physical and mental strength – both are as important as each other.

Putting aside your fears and committing to a steep climb can be nerve-racking. Walking in a bitterly cold blizzard for hours is a true test of mental strength and determination. You feel cold and tired, and want to stop or give up. You could easily give up or you could soldier on to your planned destination. Without any doubt whatsoever, I believe mountaineering is worth every discomfort and danger that is thrown at me.

Taking into consideration all the dangers and discomforts, I still want to go back for more. Even after hours of staring at my computer screen trying to describe *why* I keep going back to the mountains for more, I simply can't. I suppose my inner compass, as Alvah suggests, is truly mysterious.

My experiences in the mountains affect my everyday life in a really positive way. Escaping the prescribed city lifestyle and everyday repetitive routines helps me relax and I always have time to clear my head of any worries I might have.

Even before my accident on Mt Ruapehu, I felt lucky to be alive and to have experienced the awesome sport of mountaineering. All those little niggles that some people get annoyed with, like having a bad night's sleep, having a small blister or sore muscles, eating something you don't like for dinner – all of these things seem ridiculously irrelevant to me, as I know things can be much worse in the mountains. My living conditions are excellent compared to a lot of people around the world who live in poverty.

Overall, I think my perspective on life has been levelled and well rounded due to the things I have experienced when mountaineering.

A part of Alvah's quote reads: *We are compelled to travel in order to know ourselves and, in doing so, call our lives complete.* Through mountaineering I have discovered more about myself than any other sport I partake in. I've learnt how much the human body can be physically and mentally stretched beyond what I believed was ever possible. I never used to think I could walk and climb for over twelve hours. Now I believe I could walk for twenty-four hours, if I had to.

I know it's possible to wake up at 2 a.m., climb for five hours, watch the sunrise from a mountain summit, climb down and then walk for another five hours, easily. While this can be physically tiring, it's also mentally tiring testing the limits of the mind.

I know that I'll be a little tired after a 2 a.m. start – but who cares?! I'll have a fantastic day, see a magnificent sunrise that I'll remember for the rest of my life, and will go to bed a few hours earlier than usual. The next day I'll be ready to go again. After doing that, anything I now come across seems like a piece of cake – just too easy!

Lying cooped up in a bivi bag (a waterproof and windproof survival bag) for close to two days in a raging blizzard might seem nearly impossible to cope with, but it's a true test of your mental strength. You might think you'd go crazy and lose the plot after an hour, but it's actually quite easy. I have been in that situation. Yes, it's a little uncomfortable at times, but I'd rather be uncomfortable and safe, than unsafe and dead. After my experience in a bivi bag for two days I realised how mentally tough I could be and was surprised at how well I managed to wait out the storm.

My life wouldn't be complete without mountaineering. I wouldn't know my physical and mental boundaries. I still think I could push the limits further than I have yet. I've learnt that pushing the limits to a new level allows a great sense of satisfaction and makes the small things in life seem effortless.

At the end of the day, whether your adventure is playing sport, walking along the rocky coastline, an easy day walk through the bush or a full-on multi-day rock climbing trip, the important thing is that you're getting out there and having some fun, and doing your best. Any adventure is a good adventure. If you can see yourself having an adventure and you really want to do it, there's nothing stopping you apart from yourself. If you're passionate about your form of adventure or sport, then get out there, make the most of it, smile and have some fun.

CHAPTER TEN

A NEW LEASE ON LIFE

Bad news does not always come efficiently, rushed over the airwaves, borne by officials, imparted by grave-faced, heavy-voiced authorities. It can arrive hopelessly, messily, in painful disorder, late, distorted, and so doubly shocking.
AUTHOR UNKNOWN

26 September 2007
After I was warmed to above 32°C, I was rushed into the operating theatre and assessed by a team of surgeons. It had been fifteen hours since the Dome Shelter's door had burst open, and I had been unconscious for at least fourteen hours. I was delivered to the operating table looking as though I had been rescued from a therapeutic mud bath. Surgeons began rigorously washing and scrubbing each wound to remove the muddy grey coating that completely covered my body.

Once I was as clean as a whistle, the surgeons began the lengthy procedure of taking me to bits and then piecing me back together, minus a piece here and there.

My right leg had received far more serious injuries than I had ever imagined possible. It was severely crushed from below my knee and looked like something out of a horror movie. My lower leg near my shin area had suffered multiple compound fractures of both the tibia and fibula (both the main bones in my leg), resulting in the bones breaking through my skin and becoming exposed to the air. It's highly possible that the shin had snapped at a ninety-degree angle when it was pushed back underneath a floorboard in the opposite direction to the way I was facing. The skin around my lower leg had been torn away by the rocks that were responsible for the damage. The leg was highly contaminated with small rocks, mud and dirty water. Bits of wood were sticking out of the muscles and soft tissue. It's a wonder that I didn't quickly bleed to death and it's not clear what stopped the bleeding. It is possible the extreme pressure that the veins and main arteries were put under by the crushing force of the rocks staunched the bleeding. The extremely cold temperatures and my hypothermic condition may have slowed or stopped the bleeding. It could have been a combination of both the pressure and the hypothermia.

My right foot and ankle had been twisted under the floorboards and turned 180 degrees so that the top of my foot was twisted round next to my calf muscle. The lack of circulation caused by the crushing force, hypothermia and abnormal position of my foot meant that it was dead before it reached the operating table. With these hideously irreparable injuries, the surgeons were left with no option but to remove my dead and dying limb from below the knee. I was lucky to have no significant injuries above my right knee other than the odd cut or scrape.

Moving across to my left leg now, my big toe had been broken at the second knuckle that joins the toe to the foot. A piece of bone the size of a green pea was somehow chipped off the inner knuckle and was floating freely within the soft tissue. By the looks of the skin above the bone chip, this may have been caused by a heavy blow to the foot – perhaps a fast-moving rock. This minor fracture was the least of the doctors' and my worries.

Of great concern to the surgeons was the huge amount of

swelling that had developed around my left leg and foot. The swelling became so intense that surgeons had to perform four fasciotomies to save my left leg. A fasciotomy is an emergency procedure that releases the swelling of a limb by cutting through the skin and soft tissue with a scalpel, ending up with a deep, clean cut. If they hadn't done these, the swelling would have stopped the blood flow and my leg would have slowly died, resulting in another amputation.

The top of my foot from my toes to my ankle, the entire arch on the sole of my foot, the outside of my left leg from my ankle to just below my knee and part of the puncture wound on my inner left leg all received fasciotomies. Then the fasciotomy cuts were stitched or stapled together in the same procedure.

My inner left calf had a deep soft-tissue and puncture wound. After opening and cleaning the wound, it was the length of my hand (nineteen centimetres) and three fingers thick (six centimetres). It was at least two and a half centimetres deep. The wound reduced the swelling and my calf only needed a small fasciotomy. Luckily the bone and calf muscle were not damaged.

While trapped in the Dome Shelter I thought that my left leg looked OK. That was because my polyproplyene pants covered the soft-tissue puncture wound. I'm glad that they did, otherwise I would have passed out at the sight of it.

I also thought that my knee was either broken or dislocated. I was nearly right. My kneecap (patella) had been broken into two distinct pieces. One piece had been relocated ten centimetres up my leg, to the outer side of my thigh. The other piece sat just below where my kneecap should have been. It was at a right angle and created an unnaturally sharp angle underneath the skin – that's why I had trouble moving my knee!

X-rays that were taken while I was in between resus and the operating theatre showed my broken kneecap and big toe. The surgeons studied the X-rays and noticed my broken kneecap and toe but did nothing about it, as they were only 'scratches' compared to my other injuries.

At approximately 4 p.m. on 26 September, I came out of surgery and was taken into the intensive care unit (ICU). I was in a bad shape but had stabilised. I wasn't on the verge of death any more, however I wasn't 'out of the woods' just yet. There was every chance things could take a turn for the worse. My vital signs were closely monitored by three nurses as I slept off the anaesthetic.

Picture this: ever so slowly – as slowly as an injured slug struggling through thick mud – with no thoughts, emotions or encouragement, my eyelids began to aimlessly lift towards my eyebrows. I was beginning to wake after twenty hours' sleep. For a minute or two my brain was in neutral; going nowhere and not even thinking about thinking.

My brain slowly ground into first gear and robotically began activating my senses. All I could see was a bright pure white. My hearing was muffled, almost as if I were wearing a set of quality earmuffs. I couldn't make any distinctions between different sounds; they all blended into one. I couldn't taste, smell or move. I was puzzled and confused, yet not the slightest bit worried. Was I dead?

A vague memory entered my head, like an image flashing onto a computer screen: I was trapped in the Dome Shelter and I had died from hypothermia.

Words in my head began talking with each other: Hold on. I'm alive. I shouldn't be, but I'm alive! I think?

It became obvious that I was kind of alive. Just kind of, but I wasn't sure.

My brain started to think, No, no, I'm alive, I'm thinking. I must be alive because I'm thinking.

Eventually I battled to ask myself, a snow cave? Am I in a snow cave?

That question was answered as fluorescent lights began to appear through the bright, pure white that I had been seeing through my bewildered eyes. Everything in my field of vision was gradually getting sharper, coming more into focus.

At last my eyes came into focus, full focus. I recognised my surroundings – a hospital. I was lying on my back, arms at my side, looking at the white roof in a hospital. I should be dead – but I wasn't complaining. I had been saved, plucked somehow from the Dome Shelter and laid quietly to rest. It felt as though I had shut my eyes and been magically teleported from certain death to a hospital.

But which hospital? Where am I?

I tried to move my arms and I couldn't. I tried to check that my arms weren't tied down but I couldn't even lift my head. Neither could I move my hands one centimetre, not even wiggle my fingers. I was sure my hands had been severely frostbitten and that they'd probably been amputated.

Next I tried to move my legs, but again, I couldn't. My mouth felt odd, so I strained my eyes to look at it. From what I could see, I had tubes of some kind in my mouth, preventing me from talking. What were they doing in my mouth? Who put them there?

Out of nowhere my dad suddenly appeared. I can only remember seeing my dad's face, although he tells me he brought my mum and my friend Cameron with him. Gee, it was nice to see Dad's comforting face. Next, I'm sure I smiled at my dad, secretly hoping my injuries weren't too bad and he wasn't too upset or worried. I have never liked my dad being upset or worried; it makes me feel the same way or much worse.

Dad then began talking to me, asking how I was and telling me that I would be OK. His words and questions were carefully chosen in order to get a 'yes' or 'no' answer. I could only nod gently up and down, and shake my head slightly from side to side. The tubes down my throat prevented me from speaking.

Dad explained that I was in Waikato Hospital and that I was in the intensive care unit, or ICU for short. The ICU is a highly specialised unit that cares for critically ill people. It is the place where the hospital's sickest patients go. Twenty-four hours a day, a doctor is present, and, with help from visiting specialists, they can advise on patients' various conditions or injuries. There's always three nurses keeping a constant eye on each patient, monitoring life-preserving machines, taking notes and attending to their patient's every need.

Some patients, and I was one of them, are on life support. Life support keeps the patient's airways open and does their breathing for them to keep them alive. If this life support is turned off, the patient is unable to breathe on their own and will die.

In ICU there are patients who can't care for themselves, can't eat, can't move, and can't talk — just like me. Most patients in ICU can't remember anything about their stay; this is because of the very strong drugs that are used to reduce pain and fight infection. The drugs are so powerful that patients often hallucinate, which means they see things that aren't really there and say stupid and random things.

ICU is usually a very quiet place, with the machines sometimes appearing more alive than the patients.

I can't remember the fine details of what my dad said to me, because of the seriously strong drugs that had been administered to help relieve the extreme pain I was experiencing. I do remember Dad struggling to find the words to explain something that no words can really describe. Dad only just managed to string a sentence together that went something like, 'William, I don't know how to say this, it's very difficult for me. They had to amputate your right leg from below the knee.'

To this day, I admire my dad for being the one to tell me. I can't imagine the news being delivered by anyone else but Dad. Having the guts and strength to put aside all his own emotions and tell his son, who he loves, something as terrible as that, without shedding a tear, has got to be the most difficult thing he has ever done.

Dad knew the news would break my heart. The news was worse than that. It was a bit like having someone reach into my chest, rip out my heart, throw it on the floor and jump on it. Looking on the positive side, it was better than him having to tell everyone he knew that I was dead. But still, breaking the news of the amputation to me must have been a pig of a job.

The way I reacted to the devastating news was surprising. It surprised me then and still does now. If I had been thinking clearly, without my system full of drugs, I'm sure my reaction would have been one of sheer disbelief and panic. Instead, I calmly, quietly and peacefully thought to myself, Oh yep.

I forced a muddled smile, blinked twice, and then nodded my head, trying to say yes or OK or something like that. Still, with the tubes in my mouth I couldn't talk, and soon after, I slipped back into my drug-induced sleep.

My mum and my friend Cameron had been standing at the foot of my bed listening to my dad break the news. Sadly I either didn't see them, couldn't see them or just can't remember them – that's how powerful the drugs are.

Mum, Dad and Andrew had been at the hospital since 3.45 a.m. The time now was nearing 5 p.m. Their lack of sleep was insignificant as thoughts flooded their heads and spun wildly out of control. They now sat in the ICU waiting room in utter disbelief and shock.

Andrew was receiving so many text messages that he could not reply to one before the next one came through. The majority of messages were coming from my friends who had heard about my accident in one way or another. Some heard the news on the radio or had seen the early morning television news, but most had been told by Andrew through text messages or phone calls, as my name had not been released in any news reports yet. The details released in news reports made it easy for my friends to put the facts together – young Auckland primary teacher, two mountaineers high on the mountain, volcanic eruption – and the facts clearly hinted that James and I were in trouble. The close friends and relatives that Mum had phoned during the day had already begun to spread the news, sparking everyone's natural urge to find out more information. By sending and replying to a huge number of text messages, Andrew gradually let as many people as possible know about my accident.

Many of them have said they can clearly recall how they found out about my accident, what they were doing and where they were when they were told.

My long-time friend Laura Bateman has written her account of where she was, what she was doing and how she found out about my accident:

On Tuesday 25 September, I had spent an amazing day up Mt Ruapehu snowboarding with some of my mates. The conditions were perfect and there was not a cloud in the sky. Later on that evening, when we were enjoying a nice meal out in Ohakune, I overheard some people saying that Mt Ruapehu had erupted.

Although I knew that William and James were up the mountain climbing, I didn't put two and two together until I received the unbelievable text from my friend Matt at 6.30 on Wednesday.

'William has been badly injured in the volcanic eruption. It is not looking good. Ring me for more information.'

I automatically got on my cell phone and rang Matt

to find out what had happened. He sounded really upset, which sent me into panic mode. I raced around the house grabbing my belongings then dumped them into the car. Had I got everything? I didn't care – all I knew was that I needed to get to Waikato Hospital.

The next couple of hours were a complete blur – my phone was bombarded with calls and text messages from people who had just heard the news and I was quite glad when my phone battery finally ran out. Just before it did though, I received a call from William's brother, Andrew, to say that William needed to have his leg amputated. I was devastated when I heard this but later came to realise that this was the least of his worries.

On arriving at Waikato Hospital, I was greeted outside the intensive care unit by William's grief-stricken parents, Barry and Tracy. I don't even remember who was at the hospital at that exact moment. I just remember there were lots of hugs and plenty of crying going on. We sat in the packed waiting room staring at each other for hours before we were finally allowed to go in and see William, two people at a time.

I was not prepared for what I saw when I reached William's bed. He was attached to several different machines and had tubes all over the place. His face was swollen, his hands were cold to touch due to the hypothermia and he was barely conscious – he looked a lot different from his usual fit and healthy self.

On making it back to the waiting room, I broke down in tears. I hated seeing one of my best mates in such a vulnerable state. I remember thinking that you hear about accidents like this every day on the news but you never think it will happen to someone that you know and love. One day everything was sweet and then the next our world was being tipped upside down. This was one of the most traumatic personal experiences I and many of our friends have ever experienced.

Over the next couple of hours, we huddled in the waiting room and watched the 6 p.m. news together; even then I still couldn't comprehend what had happened. I have been tramping and climbing with William on several occasions and he is the most organised, safest person I know. Our expeditions would always be carefully planned in advance. Before setting off on our trip he would always triple check my gear to make sure I had everything that I needed. Although he was very adventurous, he did everything by the book and would not do anything that would place us in any danger. I could understand if he had been in an accident on the mountain due to his equipment breaking but I still could not believe that he had been injured due to a volcanic eruption caused by Mother Nature. I guess it was a matter of being in the wrong place at the wrong time.

About ten of our friends had arrived at the hospital by this stage, so we found some accommodation and headed back there to watch Campbell Live at 7 p.m., because they were featuring the accident. After the show we went to get some dinner and in the five minutes that it took us to arrive at the restaurant I had received seventeen text messages on my recently charged phone – all of them wanting to know how William was doing.

I was amazed at the love and support that we were receiving from our friends and family all around the world. The number of people concerned just goes to show what a popular, well-liked guy William is.

That evening we sat around chatting about what an awesome guy William is and shared stories with each other about adventures we had shared with him in the past and adventures we wished to share with him in the future. It was talking with my mates that night that helped me realise

William was strong, he was a fighter and he was going to be all right.

The majority of the next day was spent at the hospital in the waiting room. After about six hours of waiting, we were allowed to go in to see him for about five minutes. He was pretty much in the same state that we had seen him in the day before, which was heartbreaking. I sat holding his hand and talking to him, which I found difficult as I was getting no response.

The next couple of days went much the same way, with William finally waking up and being able to communicate with us through hand signals. This was definitely a positive sign and I could see that William still had his great sense of humour.

When I arrived back in Auckland, an empty house greeted me, as my parents were away. With no one to talk to, I found that I could do nothing but think about William. People would be ringing me to find out how he was doing and I didn't know – all I knew was what I was hearing on the news and in the papers, and it didn't sound good. I felt helpless being in Auckland while he was still down in Hamilton. I decided that sitting in Hamilton in the waiting room was more comforting than sitting in Auckland not knowing anything, so I travelled back down there the next day.

The next couple of weeks were spent travelling back and forth between Auckland and Hamilton. On arrival at the hospital, we never knew what state William was going to be in – some days he would be really good and then others he would have taken a step backwards. The main thing was that we all needed to stay positive, and if anyone was going to be able to cope with this situation, William was the man. He has a positive can-do attitude and was not going to let this challenge get in the way of enjoying his life to the fullest.

This tragic accident has taught me many valuable lessons, such as enjoy life and accept any opportunities that are available to you, because you don't know what is around the corner.

After a two-hour drive from Auckland, at approximately 11 a.m. on 26 September, some of my friends began to walk out of the lift onto level three and directly into the ICU waiting room. They were greeted by my heartbroken parents with arms wide open.

Each one of my friends arrived with so many unanswered questions and pieces of information passed on from one person to another through text messaging and phone calls. None of them could quite piece everything together to get the full story – it was just like an unfinished jigsaw puzzle. The missing pieces of information were soon put into place as my friends began talking to my parents and brother.

Mum and Dad had another terrible task to carry out – for those who had not heard, they had to look the first of my friends who arrived at the hospital in the eyes and break the news of the amputation and my life-threatening condition. The first few friends that they told just stared at my parents' faces, lost for words and hoping what they had just been told was not true – hoping it was some sick dream that they would wake from in the morning.

Mum and Dad delivered the latest news to each new arrival in the waiting room, while Andrew became what he calls 'the messenger boy'. Thankfully those first few friends began to text message and phone my other friends and tell them about my amputation and life-threatening condition. This relieved Mum and Dad of the horrible task of re-explaining my condition to each new visitor.

Sometime around 5 p.m., after my dad spoke to me, Andrew brought my friends in one at a time to see me in the ICU. One of the strict rules in intensive care is that you can only have two visitors at a time. Too many visitors at once might have been too overwhelming for me. Machines working to save my life took up space next to my bed and there had to be space for the nurses and doctors to get to me quickly in case of an emergency. With other sick patients nearby, two visitors at a time seemed more than enough.

Led by Andrew – the messenger boy – nervous friends put on brave faces as they gently walked into the dreaded ICU to see me, not knowing what to expect, say or do. To get from the waiting room to the ICU, they took a left turn past the lifts, then a right turn brought them to the long corridor leading up to the monitored entrance doors of the ICU. There a woman sitting at a desk sympathetically asked, 'Who are you here to see?'

A monotoned 'William Pike, please,' would have been the best reply she ever got.

Walking along the ICU corridor must have been freaky and deathly quiet, with each one of my friends gathering their thoughts and struggling to do something that no one seemed to be able to achieve – preparing themselves to see me.

What they saw must have been heart wrenching. I had visible cuts and burns on my face, arms and hand. I had an endotracheal tube coming out of my mouth to keep my airway open and keep me breathing. I also had a central venous line to administer medication into the jugular vein in my neck. I had an indwelling catheter that went up my penis and into my bladder so I could urinate at will, and cardiac electrodes on my chest to monitor my heartbeat and rhythm. On my index finger I had an oxygen saturation monitor that monitored my oxygen intake and pulse. An arterial line constantly monitored my blood pressure.

The most shocking thing of all must have been seeing

the sheet drop away halfway down my right leg. Whether or not visitors believed what they had heard about my injuries before they saw me, they sure did now – because seeing is believing.

I'm told that tears often rolled down the faces of my friends as they walked with their heads down back into the waiting room after having seen me for the first time. In the waiting room, my family and friends were in a total state of disbelief. A lot of quiet reflection on me as a person was being done. Comments were passed between each other, such as:

If anyone can do it [survive] he can do it.

I can't understand it, he [William] always crossed his Ts and dotted his Is.

If it was anyone else they might not have known what to do.

By early afternoon there wasn't a chair to spare in the waiting room, and the corridor leading up to the waiting room was lined with sad people sitting on the shiny lino floor. At every opportunity possible, information on my current condition would be exchanged between my family and friends. Every so often they were asked by the nurses to stop visiting me to allow me to have some rest and sleep. My friends were very respectful of the time that I needed to myself, but, as my mum later told me:

Everyone just wanted to be there, not one person left the ICU waiting room then – they just wanted to be there, as it seemed to everyone there was no better place to be.

Being told really bad news can shock you and bring out your emotions. When my family and friends heard about my accident, they all reacted in different ways and showed different emotions. Not everyone reacted the same way to the bad news. Some people cried, some people were sad, some were worried, some were angry and some were scared. Some people didn't show much emotion and it was difficult to say how they were feeling. It's your brain's natural response to show emotions and some people show their emotions more than others do. The important thing to remember is that it's OK to show emotions – they are your body's natural response.

Some of my family and friends had a positive outlook on my situation in the first couple of days in hospital and some had a negative outlook. People with a negative outlook were generally more sad, unhappy and worried. On the other hand, the people with a positive outlook were smiling, grateful to be talking to me and happy that I was alive. I reckon that if you have a positive attitude and outlook, and look a little harder and further into the situation, you will find something positive, even if it's something very small. Hold on to that something small, be grateful for it and cherish it.

I very strongly believe that you can find something positive from any situation. Thinking back to my first day in hospital, even though I was seriously sick I can think of a lot of positive things. For instance, I was alive. That was a bonus and a huge positive! I didn't have a bad head injury or internal stomach injuries. Only one leg had been amputated – that's better than two!

If I had received bad head injuries, I may have been mentally impaired for the rest of my life. I don't know how my family and friends would have coped with that. With internal injuries I could have had continued digestive, bowel and stomach problems – that would have been difficult to deal with.

In my situation, I thought of the very worst that could have happened: death. Luckily I wasn't dead and I tried to concentrate on all the positive things, instead of the negative things. Life had a lot to offer me and I wasn't finished yet.

I also strongly believe there is no point in worrying about

something that has already happened and is impossible to change – like my leg being amputated. Sure, it's a dreadful thing to happen but I prefer to focus on the positive things rather than the negative.

I know that talking about something that has you worried is a great thing to do. My family and friends talked to each other, and all talked to a lot of different people about what happened to me. I find that talking to someone you know really well, such as your mum, your dad, your brother, your sister or your good friends, about something that has really got you worried can be so helpful and can make you feel much better about the situation. I see talking to others as an opportunity to take the weight off your shoulders. It can be good to hear someone else's opinion or thoughts – they may see the situation in a different way to you, and perhaps in a positive way. It might make things better or it might just make things seem better than they are. Always be positive and smile. Be happy for what you have, *not* what you can't or don't have.

As I lay in a dreamy silence under the watchful eyes of nurses and doctors, the ICU waiting room remained full of nervous and panicked family and friends. News of the Mt Ruapehu eruption and my accident had been broadcast on several radio stations and television networks early on the morning of 26 September. Mine and James's names had not been released in the early morning reports. News reports said that Mt Ruapehu had erupted overnight and an Auckland primary school teacher had been badly injured.

It wasn't until the afternoon that an audio interview was held by Mary Anne Gill, the communications director for Waikato Hospital. Because of the huge media interest, Mum, Dad, my brother Andrew and my friend Cameron were recorded talking about my current condition, and my personality, and thanking people involved in my rescue. They also requested that the media wait some time before trying to interview me or my family. Before this media release, Mary Anne received over 150 phone calls and emails about my medical condition. The press statement was the beginning of an intense media frenzy. It read:

> The parents, Barry and Tracy Pike, would like to thank the media for their understanding following the accident on Mt Ruapehu involving their son William, 22.
>
> Mr and Mrs Pike and their son Andrew, 18, along with other friends and family, are amazed at William's recovery. He remains in a stable condition in Waikato Hospital's intensive care unit.
>
> They have also taken the opportunity to thank William's friend James Christie, rescuers, St Johns, staff at Taumarunui and Waikato hospitals, surgeons, nurses and doctors, particularly Dr John Bonning – the emergency department doctor who flew down to Taumarunui on the Westpac helicopter.
>
> The family are asking media to respect their privacy at this time and neither they nor William will be available to the media for at least 48 hours. If there is a change I will let you know.

Whether it was my first day in hospital or the third, I'm not sure, but between visitors I had time to think about my situation for the first time. I was extremely surprised by how sick I felt.

I thought back to what happened in the Dome Shelter. I was also surprised at how I remembered the exact details of the events that unfolded from the second I heard small rumbles in the distance until I drifted off into unconsciousness. I remembered the rocks, the water, the cold, the pain, James leaving me, preparing myself for death and then a sudden blank period. I began to wonder how I ended up in this bed. Was James OK? Was anyone else injured? These were all questions that would be answered when the time was right.

I lay staring at the roof, trying to think clearly. I could hear the droning sound of machines all around me. Mixed thoughts and feelings were crossing my mind. Calmly, without any panicking or hysteria, I began to think to myself: Am I dreaming? I hope so. This actually can't be happening. Or is it? No, it can't happen to me. Not me – I'm strong, prepared for anything and know how to look after myself in the worst mountainous environment. I'm William Pike, the William Pike who cycles, runs, swims, walks, climbs mountains and tramps through the bush. My life and my fun revolve around being active in the outdoors. I need to be fit and healthy to do those things! Most of all I need two legs!

For some reason I snapped back to reality and hid those feelings and thoughts, tucking them away in the back of my mind, to be revisited at a later date.

'This is happening,' I sternly told myself and knew I had to deal with it; I didn't have a choice.

There was no point in panicking or worrying. Absolutely nothing could be done and no amount of complaining would make my leg grow back.

I felt completely helpless lying there in such a vulnerable state. I like to be in control, not controlled. I had no say in what was happening to me, what had happened to me and what was next on the list to happen to me. From now on, whatever the doctors and nurses said or recommended was what had to happen. They knew best. I knew I was in a safe place, being cared for by incredible people, so I tried not to worry. I hoped for the best, and would try to prepare for the worst, whatever it may be.

At some point a blurry face came into my view. I knew

it was a friend but I couldn't put a name to the blurry face and just closed my eyes. I could hear someone talking but didn't reply. It was difficult to keep my eyes open so I just lay there and listened. Listening to a friend talk to me, my mind began to wander and I began to wish I had woken at 5.30 a.m. today then left the Dome Shelter with James. I wished that we were on our way to the Tama Lakes (where we had intended to camp the next night) in the Tongariro National Park, enjoying life and the beauty of Mother Nature.

The next time I opened my eyes I could only see nurses. My friend, whoever it was, had gone. I felt lonely and wished that someone I knew would come to see me.

Friends and family continued to arrive by the car load to see me. In the diary Mum kept, she wrote down the names of twenty-four people who had dropped everything and rushed from afar to see me within hours of hearing the tragic news. I have no doubt that she would have missed a few names among those frantic first few hours. I'm so grateful for having such neat, caring and loving friends and family. I've always known that I have a great family and bunch of friends, but from day one they had far exceeded my expectations in so many ways. For all of my family and friends, it was just the beginning of what was to become a terrifying rollercoaster ride of emotional ups and downs that I hope they never have to experience again.

Mum and Dad left for home on 26 September at about 10 p.m. Although they wanted to be with me, they understood that there was no way they could help me. It was now up to the nurses and doctors to work their magic. Mum and Dad arrived home to find twenty phone messages on our answerphone.

Andrew decided not to go home and slept in a motel on the hospital grounds. Sound asleep and resting his mind from the constant worrying thoughts about me that he couldn't escape, he was abruptly awoken. Andrew received a phone call at 2 a.m. from the hospital's operating theatre asking him to come back to the hospital and sign a piece of paper to give the surgeons authority to operate and perform a fasciotomy on my right upper thigh, as the swelling was threatening to cut the blood circulation to the top of my right leg. It was a terrible thing for him to have to do but it had to be done because it would help save my life!

CHAPTER ELEVEN

HOTEL HOSPITAL

The power to hold on in spite of everything, the power to endure – this is the winner's quality. Persistence is the ability to face defeat again and again without giving up – to push on in the face of great difficulty, knowing that victory can be yours. Persistence means taking pains to overcome every obstacle, and to do what's necessary to reach your goals.
WYNN DAVIS

27 September 2007
My brother Andrew woke early on 27 September. He had hoped for a good night's sleep to escape the nightmare that he was part of. His sleep had been disturbed by the surgeons that he was trying so hard to forget about. Feeling that there was no better place to be than by my side or as close as possible to me, Andrew anxiously made his way across the hospital car park and up the elevator to the ICU waiting room. It wasn't long before he was surrounded by caring and supportive friends. My friends had had the same idea as my brother and stayed the night in a nearby hotel. Once again the ICU waiting room began to fill with my friends and family.

After midday the OK was given by hospital staff for people to start visiting me again. They started to visit me two people at a time. They would stand next to me, most of them saying a few comforting words and holding my hand. The only way I had to communicate with my friends and family was to wink with one or both of my eyes. I was worried that they would be worried. I tried to smile and give the thumbs up but frustratingly I couldn't even raise my hand. All I really wanted to do was hold the hand of whoever was visiting me – Mum, Dad, Andrew or friends, both girls and guys. It was comforting and it felt like I had an outside connection to escape from the constant nightmare that I had woken to.

I had been intubated since leaving Taumarunui Hospital, which meant I had a series of tubes placed in my mouth and down my windpipe to keep my airway open. With my airway wide open, a machine mechanically pumped air into my lungs and then drew the air out of my lungs. I was too sick and sedated to breathe of my own accord – I was on life support.

Visitors could see my obvious physical injuries, such as my amputation and the cuts and scrapes on my face and arms. Thankfully, most of my physical injuries were covered by bandages and sheets, hiding them from curious family and friends. Also invisible to their eyes were serious internal injuries and conditions that I had suffered from or was about to suffer from. None of them knew the full details of my injuries, how they had occurred or what would happen next.

The doctors predicted that I would suffer from acute kidney failure due to the crush injuries to my legs. Once muscle tissue has been badly crushed and destroyed, it breaks down and releases toxins into the blood supply that are harmful to the kidneys. These toxins can cause the kidneys to shut down. The job that kidneys have on a daily basis is to filter blood to make sure it stays healthy. Acute kidney failure would mean that my kidneys had shut down and were no longer filtering my blood. If this condition was not seen to immediately, my kidneys would be permanently damaged. If this happened, the only way I could be kept alive would be through daily hemodialysis. That means my entire blood supply would need to be filtered through a large and very expensive machine, which would act like healthy kidneys. The machine is as big as a standard-sized fridge and is not portable, so I'd need to spend a lot of time in hospital for the treatment.

The doctors' predictions were right. On 29 September I suffered acute kidney failure. This was a devastating blow to me and to my family and friends.

The intravenous line that had been put in a few days earlier was put to use. Once it had been drawn from my jugular vein, my blood began to be filtered through a dialysis machine. Each day my blood had to be filtered for three to five hours. The doctor's aim was to help my kidneys recover by having the blood dialysis machine filter my blood.

From the moment I was put on blood dialysis, the doctors were confident that my kidneys would make a full recovery, and I would only need to be on blood dialysis for about six weeks. Although the doctors were confident of my kidney recovery, they could not guarantee it. If my kidneys didn't fully recover, that would mean I would have to undergo blood dialysis for the rest of my life.

The thought of being tied to a blood dialysis machine for three to five hours a day for the rest of my life was worse than losing a leg. Worse than losing two legs, even. At least with losing a leg I could still lead a normal life, go on holidays and overnight adventures and not be restricted to the house or hospital.

After the blood dialysis began, it made no difference to the state I was in. I was usually asleep, lying still all day. I had heaps of tubes and intravenous lines coming out from different parts of my body, so the blood dialysis went on unnoticed.

Towards the end of my seven-day stay in intensive

care, the doctors and nurses revealed the full details of my injuries to my family. They classed my accident as a 'multi-trauma', which meant I had suffered sudden and serious life-threatening injuries. My condition was no longer life-threatening, however it was made clear to my family that at any time it could become so.

My family and friends weren't the only people talking about what had happened to me. The eruption on Mt Ruapehu had attracted a lot of media attention, and people from all around New Zealand were interested. Newspapers, radio and television showed a huge interest, and all wanted to cover the story. At this time, the hospital's communication director, Mary Anne, shielded my family and me from all media enquiries and interviews.

Mum and Dad spent time talking to me and told me about the media interest. They asked whether I would mind if they gave the newspaper a few photos of me climbing. They also wanted to know if it would be OK if a photographer came in from the local newspaper to take photos of me. I didn't mind what happened; I was happy with whatever my family felt comfortable with. I was in no state of mind to make any decisions.

Whenever anyone came to visit me, Mum would get them to write in her diary. She made it clear that it wasn't optional – if you came to visit me, she would hound you until you wrote something in her diary! It didn't matter what it was, just a few words would be OK. At the end of each day, whether I was asleep or awake, Mum read to me the comments of encouragement and support left by those who loved me most.

Late one evening, Mum read me many little comments friends and family had written. The comments brought more than one tear to my eye and I had to ask Mum to stop after the third one.

Well, my courageous young nephew,

Life is full of defining events and sometimes you don't know that until they pass. Not so this one. Never forget that: first you should not have survived – but you did because of who you are; second, you will fight this hurdle like you have all the others – and win. We know that, like Ed [Hillary], you'll 'knock this bastard off'. Oh, and one last thing, we are always going to be here for you.

Your adoring Uncle and Aunt x

Hey Pike,

You gave us one hell of a fright mate!

I have been in to see you a couple of times and you are looking good. I have enjoyed being with you – whether our communication has been hand signals, talking or comfortable silence. You had an itchy nose the other day but you refused to let me scratch it for you – that shows your determination. Your strength is amazing and I am stoked with the progress you have made. The amount of support we have received has been outstanding which shows what a great guy you are! Love you heaps and I'm here for you whenever you need me. ☺

Love from
Laura

Will brother, I am not one bit surprised at how well you are doing. You are strong mentally and physically and we will be doing all the things we have dreamed of very soon mate. This is just a wee hurdle in the grand picture and I'll do anything to help you get back out there doin' it again!!!

Stay strong mate, your mate and fellow adventurer.

Cam 29/09/07

On 1 October, doctors and nurses announced to my mum that my condition was improving and I would be transferred to ward six and placed in a single room. This was seen as a huge forward step because I had skipped the high dependency unit (HDU). Most patients go from ICU to HDU, then to a ward.

Mum wrote in her diary:

> Quite different in ward 6 – single room and William 'is special' [because I was the sickest patient on the ward]. Pain no good 9/10.
> Doctor came in to change painkiller, it is as if William is on another level – tucked away in pain – withdrawn to cope. xxxx That's okay – he can.

I was unaware that I had been moved from ICU to ward six. The drugs I was on really did have me on 'another level', as Mum has written.

Lying on the crisp hospital sheets with my eyes tightly shut, one thing was always on my mind: extreme pain. Nurses and doctors often asked me for my pain score. A pain score is given on the amount of pain felt, with one being very little pain, and ten being the worst pain you have ever felt. In those first few weeks my pain score often topped eleven! I had never experienced that level of pain or imagined that amount of pain was possible.

My time spent in ward six was short lived. I lasted only two days, as due to other patient requirements, the nurses couldn't cope with the high level of care that I needed. It wasn't fair on the wonderful staff and my condition had slowly begun to worsen. The only option was to send me to HDU, where the level of care was a step above the care needed in a ward with one nurse for each two patients. In HDU, my pain level, injuries and general needs could be monitored more often and more quickly than in a ward.

On 3 October I was transferred to the HDU and I have no memory of being transferred. The ten days I spent in the HDU is the period of my hospital stay that I remember the least about. I do remember seeing the odd face of my close friends and family, but that's about it.

When I think back to my situation in those first few weeks in hospital, I'm so glad that I was knocked out on painkillers. Ninety per cent of the time I was in a surreal dreamland, hoping I would wake up to find everything back to normal. I wanted to look down at the sheet covering my lower body and see both my feet pushing it into the air. That wasn't the case; the sheet covering my lower body dropped to meet the mattress just below my right knee. This was a truly disturbing sight that has been etched into my mind ever since the first time I saw it.

Inside my barely functioning brain, I knew I was a very sick person. It was no secret. If I wasn't in a serious condition, then nurses and doctors wouldn't be keeping a watchful, life-preserving eye on me every second of the day and night. Friends wouldn't come to visit me with teary eyes, family members wouldn't have flown up the country to be here or be planning to fly from overseas to visit me.

My mum was booked into a hotel within walking distance of the hospital and she slept there each night, as no one can stay in HDU with a patient. Before my accident Mum had worked as a bank teller. Mum was very grateful when the Westpac Bank granted her special leave to be at the hospital with me. Westpac told Mum not to worry about her job. They would hold her position open until she was able to return to work – whenever that might be.

As soon as Mum woke in the morning, she'd have breakfast and walk up to the HDU to see me. For the whole day Mum sat next to me, read books, rubbed and massaged my back, talked with visitors and wrote down everything that took place each day in her diary. She became a second set of ears to help me understand what the doctors were telling me and what might happen next. Mum also had to be with me to give written authority for all operations.

My dad and brother took time off work over the first few days I was in hospital but were unable to stay with me every day because of their work commitments. I was very understanding of their needing to be at work and didn't expect them to stay with me all day long. Each day I'd get a phone call from Andrew and Dad asking how I was. They would always talk to Mum and get a full update on my progress. If I was awake and could talk, I really enjoyed the short conversations we had. In the weekends Dad and Andrew would make the two-hour trip from Auckland to be with me over the weekend. That would give Mum a chance to drive back to Auckland and have some much-needed time out.

Apart from the pain, the other thing that was constantly on my mind was the dryness of my mouth and tongue. Since my kidneys weren't working and I was still on blood dialysis, I was only allowed to have 250 millilitres of water per day. That included the water content in any food I ate, which was a lot. Being on an oxygen mask or having tubes administering oxygen twenty-four hours a day can seriously dry your mouth out.

For weeks I was only allowed a few sips of water each day. It nearly drove me nuts – usually I'd drink three or more litres of water per day! I could have easily secretly sculled litres of water when no one was watching but that would have made my kidneys worse. I was prepared to do anything to save my kidneys, no matter how bad it felt at the time. An intravenous drip in my arm provided me with saline solution through my blood to keep my body from becoming critically dehydrated.

My mouth and tongue became so dry that they began to crack, just like dry skin does. At times I could peel the dry skin off my tongue and flick it onto the hospital floor – I found that amusing. After desperately thinking of a way to moisten my mouth, I finally thought of an idea. I got my mum or nurses to give me a glass of water and a big cup. I constantly took sips from the glass, swirled it around my dehydrated mouth and then spat it into the cup. I did this over and over, all day long, to try and keep my tongue from peeling.

Nurses gave me a paste, like moisturiser, for my tongue, but it wasn't as good as my water trick. The paste tasted foul and through reading the list of contents I found that it contained potassium. Potassium and salt were two things that I had to avoid eating or drinking – they were bad for my kidneys at this stage. Even though I was very sick, I still had the determination to ensure that I was doing everything possible to help me recover. I liked to double-check what the nurses were doing, ask them questions and question anything that I ate, drank or had put into me via an intravenous drip. Everyone is human, we all make mistakes and I was dead set on making sure no mistakes were made that could cause something bad to happen to me.

Much to the disappointment of the surgeons, doctors, my family and me, over the past few days my right stump had been developing gangrene. Parts of the stump had turned black and it began to smell awful. The infection spread and I developed chronic septicaemia (blood poisoning) as well as a chest infection. Very powerful antibiotics were administered through intravenous lines, some of which the bacteria infecting me quickly became immune to. I was continually hallucinating and sweating. I always felt too hot and was in considerable pain and discomfort.

Mum wrote:

William not progressed as far as doctors would have liked. He is shattered, sweating – visiting cancelled . . . has a very high temperature – has an infection.

William dreaming calling James 'Douglas'. William says he was talking to his principal, Marilyn. William said he was in Bro'Town, on dialysis, with bros running everywhere and asking if anyone wanted to buy a bike – quite funny really, James and I were laughing on our way to bed.

Day and night, when I was asleep and awake, the 'boys' (hospital assistants) would visit patients to help them change position in the bed. I was unable to move myself around in bed, so the boys' job was to turn me every two hours. I looked forward to being turned as it was a change of position, it felt comfortable and stopped any bed sores developing. It also gave Mum, Dad or whoever was with me a chance to rub and massage my back. For hours I would be grateful to have someone rubbing my back. It felt so good and seemed to take my mind off the pain for a little while. Eventually I would ask them to stop, as I knew their hands would be tired.

At some stage in the HDU I vividly remember thinking to myself, If Mark Inglis can survive in a snow cave on Mt Cook in extreme sub-zero conditions for nearly two weeks, then I will be able to survive this horrible place for at least two weeks.

It wasn't the people or equipment that was bad, it was the combination of seriously strong drugs – both antibiotics to kill the infectious bugs that riddled my wounds and painkillers to fight the chronic pain.

I've always thought that when put in a really bad situation, I should weigh up the good and the bad. I've found by weighing up the good and bad with a positive attitude, I will come out on top and find some good in the situation – and I did.

I began to weigh up my situation by comparing it with Mark Inglis stuck in a snow cave. The positive things of my situation were: I'm not dead; I'm warm; I'm in hospital; I've seen my family and friends; I'm being looked after by wonderful doctors and nurses and things could be far worse. The negative aspects of my situation were: I had lost my right leg; there was a possibility I still might lose my left leg and I was terribly sick with blood poisoning from bugs infecting my wounds.

On Friday morning, 12 October, Mum was delivered the news she and everybody else had been waiting for. A doctor told her, 'I feel William has turned a corner, his infections are under control and it's time to move him to a ward.'

At 6 p.m. that day I was transferred to ward twelve and wheeled into room eleven, a large single room. When I woke up the next morning, for the first time I had an urge to inspect my body and look at my wounds.

I managed to sit up with help from Mum and a nurse. Inspecting myself carefully I found a few minor cuts and scrapes on my face, lower left back and on my right elbow. Neither I or any of the doctors or nurses could be 100 per cent sure of what caused the small burns or corrosive (like acid) injuries that were scattered on the right-hand side of my face, right arm, right hand and the right side of my back. The burns looked like they had been caused by the kind of hot orange sparks that fly from metal that is being cut or welded. Personally, I think they were burns from the sulphur that was spewed out from the crater lake. I suspect the sulphur was hot or corrosive when the shelter's door initially blew open and I stuck my head out. I think that was when I was stung on the right-hand side of my face and body. It's a mystery why the rest of my body didn't get terribly burnt.

Doctor and nurses couldn't explain another condition: my left hand had a strange tingly sensation. After talking with a few doctors, the most likely explanation they gave me was that the profound hypothermia had somehow altered the nerve sensation. It wasn't the most pleasant feeling and it was difficult to perform the simplest of tasks with my fingers, such as using a knife and fork.

I had one chance to look at my severe injuries each day when my dressings were being changed. Dressing changes were what I began to dread most. While I was in the HDU the doctors had taken a skin graft from my upper inner and outer left thigh. The skin was used to cover the soft-tissue wound on my inner left calf and on the stump of my right leg. The skin grafts were painful and felt like someone was holding a hot iron against both sides of my left thigh. Changing the skin graft dressings took at least one hour. An additional half hour was required to change the dressing on my inner left calf. After each dressing-changing session the sheets on my bed had to be changed because they were soaked in saline solution and blood.

The next dressing to be removed was the one covering my left knee. The knee had been operated on while I was in ICU. Again, after being moved to the ward was the first time I was able to sit up and inspect the injury. It wasn't much to look at, just a neat incision that had been stitched up. I was surprised at how something so neat could be so painful. Each time I tried to move my leg, my knee would hurt first and then my foot would throb. If I wanted to move my leg at any time, it had to be lifted for me, as I had absolutely no control of it.

Once it wasn't covered by a dressing anymore, I counted the sixty-four staples up my outer right thigh. The staples started at my knee and continued up to my hip. This wound, which was soon to be a huge scar, was the result of the fasciotomy that took place the night my brother was woken and asked to come into surgery to sign a form.

The remaining fasciotomies on my foot and outer leg were without dressings, all healing nicely and stitched up.

Up until now there had been great concern over whether or not my lower left leg could be saved. Doctors now assured me that it would be OK but were unsure of how much feeling would return to the leg and foot. Sitting up in bed and looking down at my lifeless left foot, I became greatly concerned. I couldn't lift it off the bed, move my toes or even feel the foot, yet it was terribly painful. With the help of a special boot on my foot, pressure sores on my heel from resting it on the bed were successfully avoided.

In the last operation performed on my stump, surgeons had applied a vacuum dressing. Don't think of a household vacuum cleaner sucking the life out of my leg, no – it's very different. It was a clear plastic dressing that wrapped around my stump and up past my knee. The dressing was airtight, with a small tube at the tip of the stump where fluid was gently extracted with minimal suction. The fluid travelled down the tube and into a small container fixed to the base of my bed. If anything was going to gross out a visitor, it would be the small container full of what I called 'stump juice'. Stump juice was a mixture of blood, bodily fluid and yuck fluid from the stump.

The time came when the vacuum dressing needed to be removed. I wasn't looking forward to it and requested some additional painkiller. The morning of the removal, a nurse wheeled in a big cylinder, slightly bigger than my scuba diving cylinder. It was full of nitrous oxide, better known as laughing gas. I began sucking on the regulator immediately and my head was soon sent spinning in circles. I wasn't laughing hysterically as you might think, instead I literally felt funny. In a roundabout kind of way, I was laughing inside my head, not laughing out loud. I managed to ring my friend Matthew Harrison on my mum's phone, and he happened to be in a library studying. I wanted to talk to him and crack some funny jokes but he was restricted to only a quiet 'yes' or 'no' for fear of being kicked out of the library!

A young trainee nurse was asked to help with the removal of the vacuum dressing. Her job was to hold my leg up in the air while two other nurses worked at removing the dressing. An hour later, without too much pain, the dressing was removed. The trainee nurse let go of my leg and said, 'OK, William, you can put your leg down on the bed now.'

'I can't,' I said with a troubled look on my face. 'It's stuck.'

'What do you mean it's stuck?' the trainee nurse asked.

'It's stuck, I can't move it, and it won't go down to the bed,' I replied.

The trainee nurse looked worried and didn't know what to do. She approached one of the registered nurses across the room and began to explain my problem.

When the trainee nurse returned with the registered nurse I said, 'Nah, just joking, I was having you on!' and then I burst out laughing.

The look of relief on the trainee nurse's face was priceless. I'm sure she would have slapped me if she was allowed to!

On Saturday 13 October, Dad wrote:

> An early start this morning!
> Off to theatre. Thinking of you as always. I stayed the night with you last night. The nurses altered your boot every two hours ... you said you had a good sleep – while you are in theatre I shall go for a walk with Mandy around the lake.

Dad slept next to me in a La-Z-Boy. He said he had a good sleep too. I wouldn't have if it were me – I prefer a bed!

The operation on 13 October was to take another skin

graft and use the skin to close the end of my stump. Doctors explained to me that as the stump was at the moment, it wasn't suitable for a prosthetic (fake) limb. There wasn't enough healthy skin to be pulled over the stump and then stitched up. By closing the end of the stump, it would give the plastic surgery team time to think about how they might make the stump suitable for a prosthetic limb. If the plastic surgeons couldn't come up with a suitable plan, it might mean that my stump would be shortened to the knee or above the knee – called an above-the-knee amputation.

On Monday, 15 October I woke up to two bright-eyed and bushy-tailed female physiotherapists, a hospital photographer and two nurses.

One of them said, 'Wakey, wakey Mr Pike, it's time for you to stand up today.' This should be interesting, I thought. I hoped I'd be able to stand.

Standing up for the first time had crossed my mind once or twice over the last few weeks and I hoped that it would go well. When I sat up in bed, I could already feel the blood rushing down to my legs. I felt light-headed.

The physiotherapists brought a frame with supports to rest my elbows on once I was standing. Before I had too much time to think about how I was going to stand on only one leg, I was scooped up by the physiotherapists and nurses. Mum looked really uncertain.

With a heave-ho from the physiotherapists and nurses, I was held standing upright. I felt dizzy and sick. The flash from the photographer's camera went off in my face a couple of times. The only good thing was that I was taller than the physiotherapists and nurses.

Thirty seconds was all I managed to stand for, but it was a start, and I was determined to stand for longer each time.

Saturday, 20 October will always be a special day for me. Just after 8 a.m., as usual, a team of doctors crowded into my room. They happily told me that based on my blood test results I no longer needed to be on dialysis! My kidneys had made a full recovery! A huge smile grew on my face and I struggled to hold back the tears. I was overjoyed and totally relieved. Mum reached for her cell phone (her first cell phone – she didn't know how to work it) and began to (or tried to) text family and friends – what great news!

As on every Saturday and Sunday, I was inundated with visitors that day. Having visitors was very tiring for me and holding a conversation became difficult towards the end of the day. After repeating my story to each new visitor, I felt like I needed a tape recorder with play-back mode for them to listen to instead of me being a parrot. However, there was no way I would ever turn down visitors and I thought every visitor deserved to hear the full story. Visitors brightened up my day, helped me stay positive, and took my mind off hospital and pain. Even if it was the 'rest period' for the ward and the 'no visitors' sign was up, I'd make sure Mum, Dad or whoever was with me would quietly sneak visitors into my room.

On more than one occasion, random members of the public would come and visit me. It was very touching to think that strangers wanted to know how I was doing. Of the ten or more strangers that called in to see me, half of them were amputees. The best thing was some of them walked in with long pants on and I could hardly believe it when they hitched their pants up and exposed their prosthetic leg!

Nurses from ward twelve offered to move me across the ward to room seven. It had a view of the lake and parts of Hamilton city – it was like a penthouse suite compared to the room I was in, which had small windows and a view of boring brown rooftops. I took up the offer without hesitation. It took Mum and a few nurses half the day to pack up my room. There were so many cards on the walls, food packages people had left me and bits and pieces here and there.

Once I was in my new room I had a visit from the plastic and trauma surgery teams. They explained to me that they had a plan to close my right stump and make it suitable for a prosthetic limb – fantastic news!

Before they operated they needed me to get healthier and stronger, as the operation would be huge. I needed to be clear of all infections and my blood results needed to show that I was eating well and generally improving, rather than deteriorating. The chances of a successful stump operation would be much higher if I was healthier.

I was prepared to wait as long as it took me to get healthier by eating a balanced diet and having special protein drinks to repair my body from the inside out. I was also prepared to wait for as long as it took the plastics team to decide how to make my stump suitable for a prosthetic.

As an amputee, having a knee has so many advantages over having an above-knee amputation. It's easier to walk up steps, down steps and up slopes and you can move the leg voluntarily. Having a knee would benefit me so much more when tramping, climbing and cycling. I wanted so badly to keep my knee. Time would tell whether or not it was possible and that's what the plastic surgeons wanted – time.

At 10.15 a.m. on 25 October I had my first shower since 23 September! Tony, the friendly hospital assistant, taped plastic bags around my legs and over my wounds. Sitting under the steaming hot shower was such a great feeling; I felt more like a human again. Since that day a hot shower has meant a lot to me. Before that shower I felt that doctors and nurses could tell if I was in my room or not by just sniffing the air!

Hospital life was getting pretty good. The trauma team of doctors told me that I was no longer their sickest patient. That was pleasing to hear!

One of the trauma team doctors, Neil Lowrie, casually

said to me, 'I've lost all interest in your blood results.' That made me laugh and was awesome to hear.

I was free of feeding tubes, catheter and all intravenous lines *and* I was clean. At last I wasn't restricted to my bed, and I was even given a wheelchair to use. Trouble!

Tony the hospital assistant was a little worried and gave me his cell phone number in case I got lost or into trouble in the wheelchair.

The first thing I did in the wheelchair was go outside. The sunlight on my face and the wind messing up my hair and bushy beard felt incredible. Just being outside made me feel confident that at the end of my hospital stay I would be OK. I could see a very small light at the end of the tunnel.

I managed to find my way back to my ward without calling Tony. Before I got back into bed, I decided to start some training. I wanted to get fit again and this was my first opportunity to begin so I went for it. I made good use of the long, straight corridors by doing laps in my wheelchair, up and down the corridors, until my arms felt like jelly and I was ready for a lie down.

Over the next few weeks I did my best to eat like a horse and train with the determined attitude of an Olympic athlete for my daily sessions of physio. Daily physio was the highlight of my day because of the friendly physiotherapists and the positive feeling I got from doing some exercise. To begin with physio was a real struggle and I could only manage fifteen minutes a session. Standing for twenty seconds on one leg was a big achievement, but it hurt as the blood rushed to my left foot and stump.

Mum still spent each day with me in hospital. She slept on a mattress on the floor of my room each night. Because I was becoming more active, the level of care I needed from the nurses changed. The nurses were doing a fantastic job, but I could do so much more now, and Mum helped me out whenever I needed it. Mum could easily attend to simple things like getting me a drink of water or something to eat, passing me my laptop and getting me in and out of my wheelchair without me needing to bother the nurses unnecessarily. Besides, they had patients to look after who were far sicker than I was, and I preferred the nurses to help them with important stuff, instead of passing me my laptop!

Over the following weeks I began to feel stronger and healthier. I even felt like going home. My pain relief was reduced to the tablet form of morphine, Panadol, and tramadol.

Now I was off the mind-altering intravenous drugs, I could rationally think about my experience. I felt sad about losing my leg but knew that it wasn't as big a deal as it had been made out to be. I was still alive, and my injuries could have been much worse – I was one lucky boy! I thought about the amputees I knew of and how they could still play sport and climb mountains. Really, I had come off pretty well considering the circumstances I was in.

Only two thoughts played on my mind. The first was the success of the operation to make my stump suitable for a prosthesis – I hoped that the doctors could work their magic once again. I didn't want to end up with an above-knee amputation, as that would considerably limit my ability to climb and tramp. My second thought was that until I actually had a prosthetic leg of my own, and had successfully climbed and been tramping, then I couldn't be 110 per cent sure that I would be able to do it. Until that moment, I would have a certain amount of doubt of whether I could or couldn't. But, as I like to think positive, I'd say I'll be fine, hopefully.

As I started to feel better I began looking through Mum's diary. The thought of the next operation always loomed in the back of my head, but reading comments like this helped:

> Pikey,
> You're a bloody legend.
> This ranks 110% on my shitometer,
> but you rank 120% on my meter of life.
> Pete Broome + all the water polo community.

Comments like these temporarily shut out the thoughts of future operations and put a smile on my face for the rest of the day. Having so much support from people made me feel full of life, and increased my certainty that everything would eventually be OK. It made me think that once I left hospital, I *would* get back to doing all the things I love.

November 7 was the date set for the operation to reconstruct my stump. The plan was to take a 'free flap' of skin and soft tissue and a skin graft from my left upper thigh. The free flap would be transferred onto the end of my stump. Nerves and an artery would be joined from within the existing stump to the new free flap. The free flap would provide sufficient cushioning for when a prosthesis was fitted and the skin grafts would cover up any remaining soft tissue. The operation was very delicate and involved microsurgery – taking anywhere from six to eight hours.

There was a five per cent chance that the operation would be unsuccessful, with the possibility of the free flap not 'taking'. My plastic surgeon asked me if I was a smoker.

'No way – of course I'm not,' I replied.

'That's good, otherwise we would have second thoughts about attempting the operation,' said my plastic surgeon.

That just goes to show how terribly harmful smoking must be for the body, I thought.

I moved from ward twelve, the general surgery ward, to

ward seven on 5 November. Ward seven is a specialist ward that cares for patients who were having or have just had plastic surgery.

I was amazed at the huge single room I got put into. There was so much room: more than enough for Mum to sleep there at night; enough for my wheelchair and walking frame; and even a few spare seats for visitors. The room looked quite bare initially, but before the day was over Mum had used medical tape to stick over fifty cards on the bare white wall – it soon felt like 'home' again.

Reading cards on the wall and browsing through the mountain of cards that Mum had filed into Clearfile pockets, I came across a hoard of cards from children I had taught. I couldn't help feeling that lump in the back of my throat and my eyes welling up as I read them:

Hi Mr Pike
I hope you are ok!
    I, well, we all miss you; we can't wait to see you again!!!!!!!
    Matthew said that there is always another mountain to climb, the mountain of recovery! Go room 17.
    I miss you Mr Pike we need to do more of your math and we need to do your sports in the lunch time!!
    Well I hope you get better soon Mr Pike.

Lots of love
Eilish

HELLO MR PIKE
It is Georgia D here from room 3.
I find it a bummer that you are in hospital
because now us seniors don't have lunch
time sport while you are away!

On Bebo, my friends and I have
created a club supporting you and
we only made it in the holidays,
now we have over 100 fans!
So that shows how much we miss you Mr Pike.
I hope you get well soon.

From your number 1 fan and misser . . .
Georgia D

To Mr Pike

GET WELL SOON
You need to get back on the mountain soon.

From Sam G (Rm 5) and
Anthony G (Rm 12)

I woke at 7 a.m. on Wednesday, 7 November. The operation to reconstruct my stump was set for 8.30 a.m. As was usual before an operation, I wasn't allowed any breakfast. I waited nervously in my bed. Before being wheeled off to theatre, I sat in a chair on some scales. I weighed 65 kilograms! This was fifteen kilograms lighter than I was before the accident – it was hard to believe.

I waved goodbye to Mum as a hospital assistant slowly wheeled me away to theatre.

'This is going to set me back three or four steps but will also step me forward an infinite number of steps once I'm all healed up,' I told her.

Six hours later I woke up with the sorest right shoulder that I have ever experienced. My pain score was a nine out of ten and I couldn't even feel the stump that had been operated on! Maybe that was a good thing.

Immediately after the operation the surgeon came to say hello.

'What on earth have you done to my shoulder? You didn't operate on it did you?!' I asked him.

He just laughed and apologised. He said it was to do with the position I was in on the operating table. I had been lying on my shoulder for six hours! Ouch!

The next day, 8 November, I woke up feeling disgusting. I ate baked beans for breakfast and then violently spewed them all over the floor. My leg wasn't sore after the operation – it was the drugs making me feel bad. I couldn't focus on the wall two metres from me and the wall sometimes spun around in circles. I was continually sweating all over my body, drenching my sheets. I had never, ever, ever felt that sick before, not even in ICU.

I discussed my problems with the doctors and nurses and they put it down to too much medication. The anaesthetic for my operation the day before and the huge amount of drugs I was on to numb the pain had worked too well and had begun to numb my brain!

After a few days I eventually came right as the drugs left my system and I began to feel clear-headed again. On Tuesday 13 November I had a superb surprise. I was daydreaming and looking out of my window while stretching my left leg with a large physiotherapy rubber band. I looked over my right shoulder and my Aunty Linda walked in my room holding a towel.

She said something like, 'Here William, do you want a towel?'

We hugged and were both overwhelmed with tears of joy. She had flown all the way over from America to see me. We get on so well and seeing her in front of me couldn't have made me any happier – it was amazing. She spent seven wonderful days with me before returning home – they were easily the best seven days that I had while I was in hospital.

The final few weeks in hospital passed quickly, with

each day being much like the one before. They all went something like this: wake at 8 a.m., have a short visit from doctors, breakfast, a visitor, shower, physiotherapy, another visitor, dressing change, lunch, a rest in bed, another visitor, dinnertime, sleep.

It seemed a little strange that I'd be leaving for home soon. I was looking forward to the smell of my own clothes and being in my bedroom. I could picture it in my head. Mostly I was looking forward to being in my own home, relaxing without a single worry on my mind and taking as much time as I needed to get back onto both feet.

On 22 November a meeting was held in my room with the relevant departments to ensure that all my needs would be met once I arrived home. The trauma team, plastic surgeons, physiotherapists, occupational therapists and ward seven's charge nurse were all present. A plan was put in place for me to leave hospital the next week!

On 27 November, two days before I was due to go home, the wire in my left knee began giving me some trouble. The wire seemed to have moved and was poking upwards underneath my skin. It became painful and stopped me from doing physiotherapy. I was gutted! I needed an operation to fix it and quickly. I wanted to go home!

The night before the operation, Mum and I went out to the car to make sure I could actually get into it and go home. My left knee had to be fully extended and we thought it might be a bit of a squeeze. We escaped from my room at dusk and I wheeled myself through the car park to Mum's car. It was a bit of a struggle to get in and out but it was possible. I would have been devastated if I had gone to get into the car and I couldn't do it!

I talked with the trauma team and they managed to pull a few strings and slot me into the operating list on 29 November. I had planned to be home by then but things don't always go to plan! I was happy enough with plan B: the orthopaedic surgeons were going to do a quick fifteen-minute operation to 'bury the prominent wire'. Luckily a local anaesthetic wasn't considered and I would be put to sleep with a general anaesthetic – just as with every other operation. There was no way I wanted to be awake when they 'buried' wire in me with some sort of hammer-like instrument.

When I woke up after the operation, it felt like I had just taken a quick nap. When I got back to my room I munched on Marmite and cheese sandwiches. Mum had brought me a block of tasty cheese – it was divine. For dessert I had lemon cake. I was used to lemon cake, and looked forward to it each day in hospital. Mum didn't buy it or bake it and the hospital didn't make it; a complete stranger made it for me and my visitors. After I left HDU, the mysterious 'cake lady' would bake a cake and drop it off in my room every week. For the first few weeks I didn't get to meet her, as I was either out of my room being operated on or asleep. I was significantly moved by Cynthia Ronaldson's kind lemon cake baking. Cynthia, what a truly amazing and likeable woman you are. You are one of the people who continually brightened my stay and attitude in hospital.

My last night in hospital was like every other. I lay in bed and thought about my entire stay there. It was hard to believe I had been in hospital for nine weeks! Every day I had something to do – there wasn't a boring moment. I only watched television twice. The first time was the rugby world cup and the other time was to watch the news.

The care from the doctors, nurses and hospital staff over the entire nine weeks was first-class. The hospital food wasn't too bad either; I had eaten much worse food when mountaineering or tramping!

CHAPTER TWELVE

HOME SWEET HOME

'Whatever life's challenges you may face, remember always to look to the mountain top, for in so doing you look to greatness. Remember this, and let no problem, no matter how great it may seem, discourage you, nor let anything less than the mountain top distract you. This is the one thought I want to leave you with.'
ALFONSO ORTIZ

Wheeling myself down the long hospital corridors for the last time seemed too good to be true. In the back of my mind I knew I'd be back for small operations – like having the wire removed from my knee – so I didn't feel a complete sense of closure. Still, I was over the moon to be leaving that place of mental and physical suffering.

At the hospital's main entry I was met by a film crew and photographer. I spoke my true thoughts to the film crew and it was on television later that night.

Outside the hospital, Mum left me in my wheelchair next to the pile of my belongings and walked through the car park to get her car. Some of the hospital staff who had been involved in my care surrounded me, saying their goodbyes and wishing me well. I probably said thank you to all the hospital staff so much that they were getting fed up with me. Still, I felt that nothing I said could ever thank them enough.

While cameras clicked away at me I thought about how

leaving hospital had been a long time coming. I finally felt like I was really going home and that it was the right thing to be doing. I was happy to be heading home to begin the next 'leg' (excuse the pun) of recovery and rehabilitation.

Mum pulled up next to me, and with help from the hospital staff, my stuff was loaded into the car. Once it was all in there was no room to spare in the boot or back seat!

Mum hugged and waved the hospital staff goodbye. It was very emotional and overwhelming for the both of us. What an amazing journey my family and friends had been through.

One goal I set myself while in hospital was to walk out of the hospital using crutches. That goal I didn't achieve. I wasn't strong enough and not completely confident at walking on crutches. So I set myself another goal. I was determined not to be wheeled, or to wheel myself, into my house in my wheelchair. It wasn't because I felt less of a person in a wheelchair or I didn't want to be seen in a wheelchair. It was simply because I had set myself a goal of not entering my house in a wheelchair and I was determined to achieve it.

On the way home my mind was ticking over with the different ways I could get into the house without the wheelchair. Stairways dominated all the entrances to my house, leaving only two options. One: have someone strong like my dad bump my wheelchair up the stairs backwards and into the house, or two: I'd have to use my crutches. I was only prepared to go with option one if I'd tried option two and failed.

Turning the corner into my street brought on a half-expected flurry of tears. I tried my best not to cry but the feeling of finally being home was too overwhelming.

Dad had surprised me by taping a large banner to the garage door that said, 'Welcome Home William' – that was very thoughtful and very special.

As it so happened, the wheelchair that had been delivered to my house was missing the correct leg and stump rests. That was very convenient, as it meant that now it was up to me to use my crutches to get into my house any way I could.

I heaved myself out of the car, steadying myself with one hand on the roof and the other on the door. Dad passed me my crutches and I began crutchering very carefully and slowly towards the back steps. I made sure Dad was behind me and Mum was in front of me in case I fell. I didn't fall. I made it all the way to the couch for a much-needed rest. Woohoo, I made it in on crutches, what a relief!

I was more relieved by that fact that my knee hadn't completely split open with the fresh stitches holding it together from the previous day's short operation!

My first night at home couldn't have been any better. I can clearly remember sitting on the couch in our spare room. I was sitting with my back against one end of the couch and both of my legs fully extended. It felt like Christmas time. Mum, Dad and Andrew kept bringing me parcels, cards, printed emails and words of support from so many people. I was grateful for a package sent to me from Penguin Books containing books on tramping and mountaineering – perfect reading material. Radio stations that I had featured on had sent me gift packs with DVDs, books and encouraging messages. I was really humbled by the amount of support that I was still receiving.

Within an hour of being home I was surrounded by many of my friends and neighbours. It was such a magnificent feeling to be back in my home environment with some of the fantastic people who had stood by my side from 26 September, when my survival was questionable, right up until this day when I arrived home.

Mum cooked everyone some yummy cheese toasties – oh how I had missed them! I sat for hours talking to everyone while they sipped on beers and wine to celebrate my return. I was happy to stick to sipping on green tea. After everyone had had enough of beer, wine and Mum's cheese toasties, they slowly left – much to my disappointment. I would have had them camp out on couches and spare mattresses if I could have – it was something special to be at home surrounded by my friends again.

Healthy fresh food, sleep and starting an exercise programme were on the top of my priority list in the first week that I was home. I was so malnourished that my fingernails had developed deep ruts in them, running from the nail bed to the fingertips. My doctor told me that a combination of severe trauma and a lack of healthy food caused the ruts in my fingernails.

Another concern I raised with my doctor was that my hair was falling out. After a shower the walls would be covered with my hair. The doctor said it was a mixture of stress and anaesthetics – not old age.

When I hopped on the scales, they read sixty-four kilograms; a mammoth sixteen kilos lighter than the day I was admitted into hospital. Of course, I had to take into account the five kilos, give or take a bit, of leg that was missing. Really I had only lost ten or eleven kilograms. But when I went into hospital there wasn't much fat on me, which meant I had lost a lot of muscle – and it sure was noticeable. My legs and upper body had almost no muscle tone. I was skin and bone.

Most days I felt good within myself, positive and happy. But sometimes I'd get a funny feeling in my stomach. I felt like I would never be the same person that I used to be, that I'd never be able to enjoy the outdoors as much as I used to. But deep inside, I knew better than to think like that. It was a stupid thought, I'm stronger than to think like that. Of course I'm the same person. My personality had not changed. I think the same. I look the same – except that my right leg has been shortened to save my life. I know my friends and family still see William Pike, nothing less and nothing more.

To begin with, every day was shadowed by pain. Sometimes the level of pain would either make or break my day. I don't like pain and I don't know anyone who does. You'd have to be as mad as a meat axe if you did. Pain is something that has haunted me since 25 September 2007. The pain is nowhere near as bad as what I had experienced in hospital but it's enough to make my mind wander and focus on the site of the pain – my stump. The only way I can describe it is a deep burning sensation. It's similar to burning your hand on a stove element, barbeque or fireplace. Initially it doesn't hurt too much, but after you have cooled it off with water it has that stinging pain – that's what my stump felt like all day long.

For the first few weeks at home, I lay in my bed for most of the day. I was so weak that I classed having a shower as moderate exercise. My daily routine consisted of waking up at about 11 a.m. and eating breakfast in bed (haha – oh yes!). I passed the rest of the day reading books, talking to visitors, replying to emails, writing postcards and beginning to write this book! At some stage during the day I made the tough trip to the lounge to do my exercises. By doing various exercises I began to build up my core stomach muscles to help with my balance and my upper body to help me use crutches. Luckily I was kept busy and was never bored.

Lying around for the majority of the day, I had a lot of time to think about my past and future goals. I thought about my personal goals before my accident. I wanted to teach full-time in 2008. I also wanted to focus on mountaineering over the 2007 winter season. I planned to build on my skill level, maintain my physical fitness and undertake several mountaineering and tramping trips, with the intention of undertaking a month-long expedition over the summer of

2007/2008. Obviously, due to my accident, those goals had been put on hold – but they hadn't changed a single bit!

My future goals are to get back into mountaineering, tramping, cycling, scuba diving, teaching and anything else that involves the outdoors – funny that. I was doing all that stuff when I had two legs! Once I get my prosthetic leg, I'll be setting many goals for myself to achieve.

For goals to be successful I believe a simple recipe is necessary. The 'ingredients' of this recipe include: a realistic and achievable goal + guts + determination + sacrifices + hard work + commitment + a positive attitude + positive thinking = achieving your goal.

There are two types of goals. One is a short-term goal and the second is a long-term goal. You need to master your short-term goals to achieve your long-term goals. Each ingredient is equally important, and each ingredient helps the others to achieve the end result.

To make it easier for you to understand my recipe for achieving your goal, I will explain each ingredient with an example.

Let's say over the past few months you have been enjoying swimming. You're not the best swimmer but you think you have what it takes to be a top swimmer. You think to yourself that one day you'd like to be the best in your school. So you set yourself a short-term goal: I want to become the fastest swimmer in my school. Great start!

Next you set yourself a goal of becoming the fastest swimmer in your city, province or area. The short-term goal is realistic and achievable. If you said you wanted to be the fastest swimmer in the world, then that's not realistic or achievable at the *moment*. However, there's no reason why it couldn't be another long-term goal. You can achieve your long-term goals by achieving your short-term goals.

To start with, you need *guts* to decide to join a swimming

school or swimming club. It takes a lot of guts to go to a new place where you don't know anyone. Don't worry, you will make new friends.

It takes *determination* to stick with your decision to join a swimming club or swimming school. You need to be determined to follow through with your goal and don't let anything or anyone get in your way. Don't worry about what other people think or say, it's your goal, you damn well achieve it.

A *sacrifice* is giving one thing up for another. To achieve your goal you will need to sacrifice some things. You might not be able to go out to a party with your friends, because you have swim training in the morning. That's a sacrifice and good friends will understand and accept that you need a good sleep to train hard and achieve your goal. Remember: don't worry about what other people think.

Training hard to achieve your goal requires *hard work*. You need to continually push yourself, make yourself hurt. As they say, 'No pain, no gain'. Always try to push yourself more than everyone else. Hard work gets results. It's the same with studying for a test. The more hard work you put in by studying, the better your results.

To be the best swimmer in your school you need to be *committed*. You need to commit to every single training. Show up early and be the last to leave. You're not going to achieve your goal if you miss trainings or turn up late. Be committed.

A *positive attitude* is so important for achieving your goals. When you think positive, you get positive. Think negative and you will get negative. You are in charge of your attitude, no one else is. By always being positive about achieving your goal, you will be one step closer to achieving it.

Positive thinking helps you believe in yourself. If you are going to achieve your goal, you need to think positively by believing you can achieve it. You need to think and dream of being the fastest swimmer in your school. Imagine yourself springing off the diving board with all your might. Dream of the water rushing past your face, with thousands of bubbles tickling your body as your arms pull through the water, and you kick as fast as you can with your feet. Think positively of your ultimate goal as you touch the wall before anyone else does, with your heart banging against your ribs and lungs desperately gasping for air. Think and dream of being the winner. Imagine it. Imagine the feeling of excitement buzzing through your body, from your toes to your fingertips, up through your heart and in your head.

When you win the race and achieve your goal, you will find out that each ingredient is worth its weight in gold when added to the recipe. All the guts + determination + sacrifices + hard work + commitment + positive attitude + positive thinking will pay off.

It's not over when you achieve your goal. Then you need to assess and evaluate your goal. You need to think what you did right and what you did wrong. Make a note of the things that went well, things that worked for you, and draw on them for your next goal. For example, what helped you achieve your goal? Was it listening carefully to the coach? Kicking faster with your feet? Putting in as much effort as you could?

Just as important as the things that went well are the things that didn't go well. Did you turn up late for training? Did you miss some training sessions? Were you tired at training from partying too much, or staying up late watching your favourite programme? There's nothing wrong with making mistakes, and only the best learn from their mistakes to make sure they don't make them twice.

After assessing and evaluating your goal, you can make a new short-term goal and a new long-term goal. After you have become the fastest swimmer in your school, it's now time to set a goal to be the fastest swimmer in your city, province or area. Then you're one step closer to achieving your long-term goal: being the fastest swimmer in the world.

Whatever your passions are, whatever sport you play, whatever you want to achieve in life, you *can* do it. Think of my recipe or devise your own ways to achieve what you want – whatever works for you; everyone's different.

Enjoy achieving your goals, enjoy life and make it fun. Live life like every day might be the last day. No regrets, no worries, no problems.

However impossible circumstances seem, with time, a good attitude and positive thinking there is a way to success. Things could always be much worse. Not all bad comes from bad circumstances and not all good comes from good circumstances. Both good and bad come from good and bad circumstances – it's just a matter of seeing more good from every circumstance.

Making the most out of what you have and not dwelling on what you don't have is the key. Also, if you see an opportunity – go for it, and, most importantly, make the most of it.

Get a sense of humour; that helps you see the good from every circumstance. Laugh, joke around, be silly – have fun. Life is boring without a laugh every day. Use humour to turn every experience into a positive and fun experience.

Enjoy the good times in life. Don't ever take anything for granted, especially your health. Take a moment when you're fit and healthy to think about how great you feel. Never forget your health is more important than your wealth.

In life, what matters most is friends and family – without them, you don't have much.

Feel lucky for who you are, where you are and what you have – you'll always be luckier than a million other people.

Lastly, if you think every day *can* be a good day, then soon you'll be thinking every day *is* a good day.

EPILOGUE

Walking is man's best medicine.
HIPPOCRATES

The date is Thursday, 20 March 2008. In five days it will be six months to the day that Mt Ruapehu erupted. Hippocrates reckons walking is man's best medicine and I'd say he's spot on. Walking – that's exactly what I have been doing for the last few weeks and I feel great.

My prosthetic limb was fitted on 20 February, one month ago. As you can see in the photos, it's a pole, not a leg look-alike. I prefer the bionic look, and apparently girls like skinny ankles.

When I'm out on the street, I'd rather people see the leg and instantly know it's fake, rather than have them staring and trying to work out if I have a look-alike or not.

The prosthetic foot has toes that are joined together and a gap between the big toe and the second toe, so I can wear jandals. The only problem is I don't have a real big toe to stop the jandals from sliding off. My dad thinks a few Velcro dots on the sole of my foot and on the jandals will solve the problem.

The socket is made from fibreglass and I wear a few socks on my stump. Initially when the fibreglass socket was cast to the shape of my stump, it had a great fit. My stump will continue shrinking for many months, until it reaches

EPILOGUE

its final shape. Until then, a few extra socks help keep the socket fitting as best as it can. Soon, I will have the socket reshaped and I will be back to one sock, until the stump shrinks a little more.

In the beginning, the guys at the limb centre told me to only use the leg indoors, and they recommended standing only, like while I'm washing the dishes. Boring!

After a week with the limb I rang Cameron and said I'd meet him at the Mt Eden quarry for a rock climb – he was keen as always.

I decided to abseil first and see how I'd go. At the top of the abseil my prosthetic got caught in a small crevice. I fell a short distance and twisted the pole off centre. I didn't hurt myself and it didn't affect my rock climbing, so once at the bottom I climbed back up to the top. What an amazing feeling of achievement that was!

The next day I went into the limb centre and told them I had absolutely no idea how the limb became twisted.

If I can rock climb after having my new leg for a week then the possibilities are endless. In time I *will* be doing everything I used to do. I realise there will be small compromises I will have to allow for, but they are a small price to pay considering I'm lucky to be alive.

The pain in my stump has almost gone completely – what a relief! I still have the wire in my left knee and it's due to be removed in a few months' time. My stump needs a small operation to tidy up a piece of skin that's folding onto itself. Both my stump and the scar on my left calf will be operated on in a few months' time. I'll be going to Southern Cross Hospital in Hamilton for these.

I'm back teaching for one day a week at a school ten minutes up the road from my house. I love teaching and wouldn't want to be doing any other job.

I have been given a second chance at life, and presented

with new and interesting opportunities and challenges. Every day that I'm alive is a bonus. I will cherish my new way of life and make the most out of whatever I'm confronted with in the future.

It's taken me just over three months to write this book. It wasn't easy, but I have enjoyed the challenge and I've enjoyed every moment of writing it.

As I finish these last few sentences I can't stop thinking about the three-day kayaking trip that I'm going on with four friends in two days time. It will be my first overnight adventure in six months – bring it on, baby!

I'll leave you with one last quote:

And so what I've learned over the last twenty [three] years is that I am the sole judge and jury about what my limits will be. And as I look toward the horizon of the next twenty years, it is no . . . no *limit.*

With that kind of knowledge, I've grown as old as I can possibly be; the ageing has stopped here, and now I just grow better.
GLORIA NAYLOR

William ☺

GLOSSARY

ADZE (ON AN ICE AXE)   a tool that's kind of like an axe except the blade is mounted at right angles to the handle. Used for chipping away solid ice and cutting steps when not wearing crampons.

AVALANCHE   when a whole lot of snow, ice or mud gathers into a mass and slides down a mountain, often taking everything in its path. This can happen really quickly and with very little warning.

BUOYANCY CONTROL DEVICE (BCD)   the jacket that scuba divers wear. A BCD has an inflatable bladder that you can add air to or take air out of in order to control whether you float or sink. BCDs usually have plenty of pockets or D-rings so that you can carry all the gear you need on a dive.

BIVI BAG (ALSO KNOWN AS A BIVOUAC BAG)   a lightweight, thin, waterproof fabric shell designed to go over a sleeping bag. A bivi bag will give you extra insulation and form a barrier against wind and rain.

CARABINER   spring-loaded metal ovals that open and close. Carabiners are used to clip pieces of gear together or to clip gear onto a rope. An essential piece of equipment when climbing with a rope.

CRATER LAKE   the lake that forms in the crater of a volcano.

CRAMPONS   a frame of hardened steel that securely clips or ties onto mountaineering boots with sharp spikes to provide traction on hard snow and ice. Crampons generally have ten points facing down and two at the front for 'front pointing' up vertical ice.

CRAY SNARE   used to catch crayfish while diving. A cray snare is a retractable wire loop on the end of thin metal tube. The wire loop goes around the cray's body and is then retracted. Acts just like a lasso.

DEHYDRATION   when you lose too much fluid through sweating, peeing, pooing or vomiting. This can be really dangerous as it can cause body functions to shut down, and eventually lead to death.

FROST BITE   damage to skin and other tissues that happens in extreme cold. When you're in extreme cold, the blood vessels closest to the skin narrow down so that the heat in your blood stays close to your vital organs. Most likely to be seen on fingers and toes. Frost bite is irreversible – usually leading to amputation.

HYPOTHERMIA   a condition that occurs when your body is exposed to the cold for too long. If your body's temperature (37°C) drops below what it needs for normal functioning, it will try to maintain the temperature of your core (your heart, lungs, liver etc). There are different symptoms for the different levels of hypothermia.

ICE AXE   An ice axe is an essential multi-purpose mountaineering tool carried by every mountaineer.

INTENSIVISTS   the hospital team that look after really critically ill people. This group includes specially trained doctors and nurses.

LAHAR A lahar is a type of mudflow usually containing mud, rocks and water that flows down from a volcano, typically along a river valley. A lahar can be lethal if you get engulfed by one. They move very fast and have the consistency of concrete.

MARINE RESERVE an area of the sea where everything – including the animals, the water, the plants and the undersea environment – is protected. You're not allowed to interfere with the marine life by feeding, touching or taking it. If you get caught doing any of this, you could end up being fined or imprisoned

NITROUS OXIDE a gas that is used as a painkiller. It also gets called laughing gas as it can make the patient taking it feel a bit silly.

O-RING a ring that is used to make sure there's an air tight seal on a dive cylinder.

OVERPANTS a pair of thin waterproof and windproof pants that go over your pants when you're climbing. They provide an extra layer of fabric against wind, snow and rain.

PICK (OF AN ICE AXE) a long, thin, sharp metal part of an ice axe used to 'bite' into the ice to climb vertical ice.

POLYPROPYLENE a light, warm, moisture wicking, quick drying, strong synthetic fabric that traps warm air next to your body making it ideal to use in the outdoors.

SADDLE a pass or ridge between two peaks.

SNOW BLINDNESS kind of like sunburn of your eyes. When

sunlight reflects off snow or ice and you don't have sunglasses, the sun's UV rays can burn your eyes. Snow blindness can range from having bloodshot or gritty-feeling eyes to your eyes swelling shut to permanent loss of vision in severe cases.

THERMALS clothes that trap warm air next to your skin meaning you're less likely to get cold. (See also Polypropylene.)

TITANIUM metal that is 30 per cent stronger and 50 per cent lighter than steel so it's perfect for using to make tools used for tramping and climbing as it means your pack will be much lighter.

WEIGHT BELT a belt that divers wear that has weights on it. This can be used to help manage buoyancy in the water due to neoprene (wetsuit) being positively buoyant.

WIND CHILL FACTOR the amount of cooling your body feels when the weather is windy or cold. The actual air temperature might be quite high but the wind chill factor can be calculated to work out the temperature you'll be feeling in the outdoors.

RECOMMENDED READING

Note: For those of you who aren't used to APA referencing, the jargon below can be very off-putting! Don't let it be. Below are some amazing, inspiring, knowledge- and advice-filled books.

Annotated example:

AUTHOR
LAST NAME, FIRST NAME
　　　　　　　　　　　YEAR OF PUBLICATION　　BOOK TITLE

Dorfman, Eric. (2007). *Inside New Zealand's National Parks.*
Penguin Books: New Zealand.

　　　WHO PUBLISHED THE BOOK AND WHERE IT WAS PUBLISHED

Allan, Stu. (2006). *Bushcraft. Outdoor Skills for the New Zealand Bush.* Mountain Safety Manual 39. New Zealand Mountain Safety Council: New Zealand.

Barnett, Shaun and Brown, Rob. (1999). *Classic Tramping in New Zealand.* Craig Potton Publishing: New Zealand.

Barnett, Shaun. (2004). *North Island Weekend Tramps.* Craig Potton Publishing: New Zealand.

Charles, Graham, Jones, Mark and Waters, Marcus. (2007). *Unclaimed Coast: The First Kayak Journey Around Shackleton's South Georgia.* Penguin Group: New Zealand.

Cotter, Guy and Sedon, Mark. (2003). *A Climber's Guide to New Zealand Mountaineering Techniques.* Adventure Consultants Ltd: New Zealand.

Dingle, Graeme. (2005). *Dingle.* Craig Potton Publishing: New Zealand.

Dorfman, Eric. (2007). *Inside New Zealand's National Parks.* Penguin Books: New Zealand.

Dufresne, Jim. (2006). *Lonely Planet Tramping in New Zealand.* 6th ed. Lonely Planet Publications Pty Ltd: Melbourne.

Fiennes, Ranulph. (2007). *Mad, Bad and Dangerous to Know.* Hoddor & Stoughton Ltd: London.

Griffin, Christine. (2004). *New Zealand Outdoor First Aid.* Mountain Safety Manual 33. New Zealand Mountain Council: New Zealand.

Haddock, Cathye. (1993). *Outdoor Safety. Risk Management for Outdoor Leaders.* Mountain Safety Manual 38. New Zealand Mountain Council: New Zealand.

Inglis, Mark. (2003). *To The Max.* Random House: New Zealand.

Inglis, Mark and Ell, Sarah. (2008). *High-tech legs on Everest.* Random House: New Zealand.

Jackson, Jack. (1997). *Top Dive Sites of the World.* New Holland Ltd: London.

Krakauer, Jon. (1996). *Into The Wild.* Doubleday: New York.

Krakauer, Jon. (1999). *Into Thin Air.* Anchor: New York.

McMurray, Kevin F. (2001). *Deep Descent. Adventure and Death Diving the* Andrea Doria. Pocket Books: New York.

Moore, Colin. (2006). *Take a Kid Outdoors.* New Holland Publishers: New Zealand.

RECOMMENDED READING

Mountain, Allan. (1998). *The Diver's Handbook*. New Holland Ltd: London.

Owens, Ian, MacQueen, Will, and Irwin, Dave. (2002). *Avalanche Accidents in Aotearoa – New Zealand*. New Zealand Mountain Council: New Zealand.

Simon, Alvah. (1999). *North to the Night*. Broadway Books: New York.

Thomson, Richard. (2006). *Tongariro. A Guide for Climbers and Ski-mountaineers*. New Zealand Alpine Club: New Zealand.

Viesturs, Ed and Roberts, David. (2006). *No Short Cuts to the Top*. Broadway Books: New York.

Worsley, Frank A. (1999). *Shackleton's Boat Journey*. Random House: London.

RECOMMENDED WEBSITES

www.alpineclub.org.nz – New Zealand Alpine Club, the home of mountaineering in New Zealand

www.divecentre.co.nz – Information on diving, dive locations and getting into diving

www.doc.govt.nz – The Department of Conservation. Great information on pretty much everything that's 'in the outdoors' in New Zealand like walks, tramps, climbs, marine activities, weather and safety

www.mountainsafety.org.nz – The leading authority for outdoor safety in land-based activities in New Zealand

www.mtruapehu.com – Comprehensive information on activities at Mt. Ruapehu

www.opc.org.nz – The Sir Edmund Hillary Outdoor Pursuit Centre is New Zealand's leading provider of outdoor education to secondary schools, and strives to develop people's potential through outdoor education and adventure. OPC runs a full range of programmes for youth and adults wanting to develop outdoor skills and experience adventure. OPC also runs programmes for school students, special needs groups, and corporate staff training

RECOMMENDED WEBSITES

www.prytex.co.nz – Outdoor Clothing and Equipment

www.rescue.org.nz – The website of the Westpac Waikato Air Ambulance and the Taupo Lion Foundation Rescue Helicopter; both of the helicopters involved in my rescue

www.adventurephilosophy.com – One of New Zealand's top outdoor adventure teams. The first to kayak around South Georgia Island. Watch these guys – they're going places!

FROM MY PARENTS

Barry Pike
Tracy and I admire and love Andrew for his devotion to William and ourselves as the weeks of hospitalisation and a whole new life were to unfold before us.

Andrew has been a loyal and devoted son, giving me immense strength and encouragement during the most difficult time in my life. We love you Andrew x

'Nothing is more beautiful than the love that has weathered the storms of life.' – Author unknown

Tracy Pike
Just so that you know –
It isn't a job –
It is an opportunity, a privilege –
It is a blessing and an adventure –
I love being your wife Barry, and William and Andrew, your mum – x